BLESSED AMONG WOMEN

In the words of Mary, the Mother of Jesus
"The woman who *could* worship her son!"

Paulette Sizemore

ISBN 978-1-64114-494-0 (Paperback)
ISBN 978-1-64114-495-7 (Digital)

Copyright © 2017 by Paulette Sizemore
All rights reserved. No part of this publication may be reproduced, distributed, or transmitted in any form or by any means, including photocopying, recording, or other electronic or mechanical methods without the prior written permission of the publisher. For permission requests, solicit the publisher via the address below.

Christian Faith Publishing, Inc.
296 Chestnut Street
Meadville, PA 16335
www.christianfaithpublishing.com

Any scripture used in this manuscript whether direct quotes, paraphrased by the characters, or the imaginary ideas of the author; have been taken from The King James Version of the Holy Bible. 1996 Broadman and Holman Publishers

Printed in the United States of America

Contents

A Note from the Author 5
In Appreciation 9

Part I. The Infant Redeemer
Chapter 1. The Conception 13
Chapter 2. Unto You a "Savior" 21
Chapter 3. The Dedication of the Lamb 30
Chapter 4. The Flight into Egypt 35

Part II. The Young Christ
Chapter 5. Memories of the Child Jesus 39
Chapter 6. The Passover 47

Part III. The Word Was Made Flesh
Chapter 7. Cousin John 54
Chapter 8. Jesus Picked Twelve 61
Chapter 9. The Ministry Begins 67
Chapter 10. Performing Miracles 76
Chapter 11. The Parables 88

Part IV. The Ultimate Sacrifice
Chapter 12. The Arrest 94
Chapter 13. The Mock Trial 102
Chapter 14. The Crucifixion 112

Part V. The Messiah Has Come
Chapter 15. He Finally Came Down 120
Chapter 16. He Has Risen 125
Chapter 17. The Young Roman Soldier 130
Chapter 18. My "Son" No More, but
 "My Lord and My God" 140

A Note from the Author

Having gone to the theater for the first time in over twenty years, and watching Mel Gibson's movie, *The Passion of Christ*, which in my opinion is the greatest movie ever made, I felt a great "passion" to write about Mary, the mother of Jesus. I had a desire to portray the pure heartbreak that she must have felt. However, having three children of my own, I can't begin to imagine the emotional pain that she must have endured the last week of her "son's" life. I hope, in some small way, this book, *Blessed among Women*, will give Mary the honor and respect that she is due for her obedience in accepting the role of becoming the "Human Mother" of the God of the Universe. She became a humble part of "His Perfect Plan" for the sin-filled human race. I think that her devotion to Father God should be an inspiration to all of us women past, present, and future.

    I will not pretend to have personally sat down with Mary, the Mother of Jesus and interviewed her for several hours on the part of her life, as having been favored by God, the Father and Creator of the Universe, to be the woman to carry in her Blessed Womb, the Precious Son of God.

    I will, however, say that I did have some divine guidance from the Holy Spirit of God to put this manuscript together. No, I am not trying to put myself on the same level as this Great Woman of God. In my opinion, that would be blasphemy. Our two experiences, although with the same Godly Spirit, were so very different. In that, she, Mary, the Mother of Jesus, was chosen by Father God Himself to become the "human mother of His Precious Only Begotten Son." I, on the other hand, can only claim the most valuable, freely given, and ultimate gift of salvation that was bestowed upon me by His Precious Son, Jesus, some two thousand years later after His "human life" on earth was over. Only through His love did I receive the help from the Holy Spirit to write this book.

Blessed among Women
In the words of Mary, the Mother of Jesus.
"The woman who *could* worship her Son!"

I would like to express my ideas of how Mary, the Mother of Jesus, may have felt thirty-three plus years of her life while watching her son, the "God Child," make His destined journey from His birth in a manger in Bethlehem to His crucifixion on an old rugged cross of Calvary. He then, after three days, arose from the dead, walked with His disciples for a short time, and finally ascended to Heaven, returning to His throne to the right hand of His Father, Yahweh, God of the Universe!

Except for a few direct quotes from the King James Version of the Holy Bible, the books of Matthew, Mark, Luke, and John, the contents in this book are entirely from my imagination as a human mother who has a son. I do not wish to take anything away from, or to add anything to the life of Mary, the Mother of Jesus. She, who is called "Blessed among Women," deserves the utmost respect. I do not, however, think of her as a "god" or that she is to be worshiped. I believe with all my heart that there is only "*one way*" to be able to enter heaven and that is—by and through the shedding blood of the Lord Jesus Christ. I also believe that we are, when praying, to pray only to Him, asking in His name and by His Will and not to pray to or through any other name. These words were also taken from scripture of the King James Version of the Holy Bible.

I, myself, have been blessed beyond measure and it is not because I have deserved anything, but simply because as the little children sing that beautiful little song; "Jesus loves me!" For this reason, I have attempted to write this book to try to show Him some praise and my appreciation for everything that He has done for me. I could never be able to thank Him enough!

Dear reader, I want to thank you so very much for reading this! I pray that you have or will receive in your lifetime, the Greatest Gift possible for man, woman, boy, or girl; and that is, the "Gift of Salvation," which can only be freely given to you from the Lord and Savior, Jesus Christ. I pray that you are richly blessed as you read this book and later throughout your entire life.

Thank you!

In Appreciation

I would like to express my utmost appreciation to the following people, my friends and family for all the patience, understanding, encouragement, and confidence that they had in my attempting to write this book.

June and Walter Henderson, my godly parents, for raising me in a truly Christian home, where I was disciplined, but I was also loved unconditionally. I was taught about Jesus while sitting on my mother's lap in our old, faded, blue rocking chair. The first little song that I remember singing is "Jesus Loves Me."

Basil Sizemore, my loving husband, for always believing that I could accomplish anything no matter what I would undertake. He has always encouraged me and had so much faith in my ability to do absolutely anything. He has helped me in writing this book, explaining passages of Scripture to me and helping me to put my thoughts into written words. I have been blessed with a good and just man who loves the Lord Jesus. He has also been a wonderful father to our three children.

Taima Sizemore Arms, my eldest daughter, who has attempted to edit my manuscript with honesty, giving her opinion no matter how critically judgmental it seemed to be so that I could see and possibly correct superfluous mistakes. She kept saying, "Mom, just try to relax, get a cup of coffee, calm down, and start over. I know that you can do it, just pray and write!"

Tonette Canaday, my youngest child, who kept telling me the entire time, "If you feel that this is something that God wants you to do, then you better at least try to get it done and done well."

My son, Walley, who said, "Write it, Mom, and He will use it for His glory!"

My eldest grandson, Landis Madron, for his support, input, and his encouraging words.

A picture of Michayla Arms, my eldest granddaughter, is on the front cover of the book along with the little two-week-old lamb that we borrowed for the picture from Tom and Terry Turbyfield, the owners of the Turbyfield Farm in Elizabethton, TN.

I thank God for all the rest of my family: all my grandchildren who have so much confidence in my ability to do anything and especially for my "big brother, Dub," ten years older than me, who always thought that I was a genius.

The many godly pastors that I have known over the years. My first Pastor, Dr. David Knight, Pastor Ronald Scarbro, and my son-in-law, Pastor James Canaday, along with so many others who have taught me the meaning of the "LOVE OF GOD"!

And I am leaving for last, the most important One of all,
My Lord and Savior, Jesus Christ.

He has done so very much for me. He freely gave me the greatest gift ever known to man; He gave His life on the cruel cross of Calvary to save my ungodly, corrupt, unworthy soul from Hell. I accepted His Gift of Salvation on April 13, 1997. That would have been enough, but then the following year, April 23, 1998, just one year after I accepted Him into my heart, He saw fit to cure me of terminal cancer. The same disease that three doctors had given me only six months to live. He answered the prayers of my pastor, Dr. David Knight, and my church family, at New Beginning Baptist Church in Knoxville, Tennessee, along with many other folks, friends, and family, who believed in the "healing power of Jesus"!

In my seventy years, I have been blessed over and over beyond measure, and it was not because I was deserving of anything at all, but simply because as my little grandchildren sing that beautiful little song, "Jesus Loves Me"! For this reason, I have attempted to write this book to try to show Him some praise and my appreciation for everything that He has done for me. I could never be able to thank Him enough!

I want to thank you so very much for reading this book! My earnest prayer is that you have already received or will receive in your lifetime, the greatest gift possible for man, woman, boy, or girl; and that is the *gift of salvation*, that can only come from the Lord and Savior, Jesus Christ. There is only "*one*" way, and that is through the shed blood of Jesus Christ.

I pray that you are richly blessed throughout your entire life.

Thank you!

Chapter 1

The Conception

Oh yes, I can remember about thirty-four years ago, I remember that day as if it were just yesterday. It was late in the evening. The sun had already gone down. I was becoming very weary because I had been working in my vegetable garden for most of the day and then I had gone to the little brook and washed some of my clothes. It had been an unusually hot day; even the wind was warm. There had been no cool breeze blowing the entire day.

I was more than ready to go to bed. As I was turning down the covers for a long night's sleep, I heard a rumble behind me. Then I beheld a bright light shining into the room, and I turned toward the door to see what the strange noise was. Suddenly, I became frightened for I saw; before me, a man clothed in white raiment the color of pure, white snow, and he was hovering about the room. This man was the most beautiful creature that I had ever seen. I knew in my heart that he had to be an angel of the Lord! As I fell on my face before him, he spoke saying these exact words:

"Fear not Mary, for thou hast found favour with God, and behold thou shalt conceive in thy womb, and bring forth a Son, and shalt call His name Jesus. He shall be great, and He shall be called the Son of the Highest; and the Lord shall give unto Him the throne of

His father, David, and He shall reign over the house of Jacob forever; and of His kingdom, there shall be no end."

I knew this could not be possible because I was betrothed to Joseph, I was a virgin, and I had never known any man. In a very shaky voice, I began to speak to the angel who had said that his name was Gabriel. I told him all the reasons that my going to have a baby would be impossible. A woman being impregnated by the Holy Ghost had never been heard of, and I thought that surely he had come to the wrong person. (At the time, I did not know that I would receive many visits from the angel of the Lord in the years ahead.) I could not understand at all what was happening and then the angel, Gabriel, spoke to me again, saying these words.

"The Holy Ghost shall come upon thee, and the power of the Highest shall overshadow thee; therefore, also that holy thing which shall be born of thee shall be called the Son of God. Behold, thy cousin, Elizabeth, she hath also conceived a son in her old age; and this is the sixth month with her, who was called barren. For with GOD, nothing shall be impossible."

I knew in my heart and soul that this thing was true, and I was no longer afraid. I knew that I must depend on God to take care of everything. Then I said to the angel of the Lord, "Behold the handmaid of the Lord; be it unto me according to your word." Then the angel Gabriel disappeared as suddenly as he had come.

I had a lot of thinking to do, so I laid down on my bed for what I thought would be a long, sleepless night of prayer and understanding. Over and over in my mind, I kept thinking of how I would be able to tell my family and especially Joseph. What could I say to them? They would never believe me and would surely accuse me of blasphemy. I realized that only Elizabeth would understand what had happened to me that night because I had heard that she also had been visited by the same angel of the Lord, Gabriel, and was told that she would carry a son who would grow to serve the Lord! I knew that after I talked to Joseph that I must go visit her.

I did not know why I was so worried because I knew that my God would not lead me into anything that He would not go ahead of me to clear the way. Still, in my culture, it was forbidden for a woman to become pregnant before marriage. She would be punished either by being stoned to death or put away from the sight of anyone and shunned as a fallen woman for the rest of her life.

I did not know how I was going to persuade Joseph that the thing I was to tell him was the true miracle of God. A miraculous virginal conception would be the hardest story for anyone to believe because of the impossibility of it all. But as the angel, Gabriel had told me, "With GOD, nothing is impossible!"

I knew that Joseph was a very just man, but he was also a very godly man. I also knew that he loved me with all his heart, but I wasn't sure just how far he would go to protect me from something that he thought was wrong unto the law of God. Joseph, of all people, would not deliberately break the law for anyone.

Being very worn out from the distressing encounter with the angel, I decided that I needed to get some sleep and trust God to help me because I knew that the days ahead would be long and stressful for both of us. I tossed and turned for a while and then I fell asleep. The morning light streamed into the room much too soon, and I had to make myself get up to start my long new day. I wanted to get to Joseph before he began his morning routine. I washed my face and hands, rinsed my mouth with cool water, and hurriedly got dressed.

I tiptoed out of the house into the refreshing early morning air and headed down the path to the little carpenter shop where I found Joseph already hard at work. He was carving the legs of a beautiful round table and softly humming a little tune as he worked. *Not for long*, I thought, *not for long!*

When I reached the little shop area, it seemed that the last few steps had taken as much time as the long walk from home. Telling my betrothed, the man I loved, with whom I was supposed to spend the rest of my life, that I was pregnant would be the hardest thing that I had ever done. The same amazing man was expected to believe my words, knowing that he had never touched me and that the story I was telling him was impossible. Suddenly, I was frightened again. I had to convince Joseph that the Holy Ghost had impregnated me. He would surely get mad at me and call this blasphemy.

As I approached, Joseph raised his hand in greeting and nodded a sweet, loving, yet questioning smile at me. I had never gone to the little carpenter shop. As I looked up at him and into his sweet face, I could feel tears building up in my eyes. I had tossed and turned most of the night wondering about how I was going to tell him and the exact words that I would say. Suddenly, before I could open my mouth, I began to cry. Tears were falling like a waterfall down my face. My body was trembling, and I felt that my heart would surely beat out of my chest.

Joseph laid down his mallet on the ground next to the table. He walked over to me, took my hand, and led me over to sit on a wooden block that was over near the back wall. Then he knelt in front of me, took both of my hands in his, and while looking into my eyes he said, "Mary, my sweet Mary, whatever could be so upsetting to you, my love? Why do you weep so bitterly? Please tell me. Please, let me try to help you! You are breaking my heart because I have never seen you cry!"

I began to tell him about the angel Gabriel having appeared to me the night before and every word that he had said and how beautiful and heavenly he was. Crying and trembling, I continued until I had told him the entire story.

Joseph listened with a sad, hurt look of disbelief on his face and in his eyes. He had known me since probably I had begun to talk and had never known or heard of my ever telling a lie, until now, of course. Still, he could not accept such a thing was true. In his mind, he could not believe the "impossible"!

He continued to hold both of my hands, and neither of us spoke a word. Suddenly, he also had tears running down his face. We just sat and cried together, and while we were looking into each other's eyes, I could see the terror building up inside him. It seemed that we had sat there forever and then Joseph dropped my hands, stood up, and looked down at me for a couple of minutes and then he began pacing the floor. I knew that he was trying to comprehend what I had just told him and to do the right thing in this weird situation.

I said "Joseph!" with a question in my voice.

He lifted his hand for me to be silent for a little while. Both of our hearts were heavy. I knew him to be a patient and honorable man, but I also knew that this was beyond his human understanding. The look in Joseph's eyes proved that his heart was broken.

Suddenly he broke the silence. "Mary, I must have some time to think about this. You must go. Please leave me now. Go home and talk to no one until I have had a couple of days to find the answers and get back to you. I need to try to decide what is best to do. I must do a lot of praying. God will provide me with the answers that I need. You must go now! Please! Just hurry home! Remember, you must talk to no one!"

The rest of the morning was long, and I thought it would never end, and I worked as hard as I could to try to pass the time, crying so hard at times that I could hardly see what I was doing. The evening dragged by, and the night was much longer. I did not ask God for help because although nervous, and at times even scared, I knew in my heart that God would show Joseph the truth and He would show him the plan that he had for our lives. After a few minutes, I fell into a very deep, peaceful sleep.

Just at the break of day, I was awakened by Joseph's pounding on my door, yelling, "Mary, Mary, get up quickly! I have good news! I, too, have been visited by the angel Gabriel! Get dressed, for today we must make haste, get married, and we shall live together and live as the angel of the Lord has ordered us to do as you carry the true Son of God! We shall call His name, Jesus, and we shall raise Him in the name of the Lord, our God!"

I dressed quickly and then opened the door. "Come in, my loving Joseph!" I said.

As he walked into the room, he took my hands in his and led me to the small chair that he had made for me the day that we became betrothed. He had me to sit down, and he sat at my feet as he had done the night before, and then he began to tell me all about his visit from the angel Gabriel.

Joseph told me that he was thinking of how he could put me away privately as to cause less scandal and not to make me a public example. He was stressed out beyond belief, even somewhat scared. He decided to try to get some sleep and think it over the next morning.

After a few hours of tossing and turning, he was finally able to fall into a deep sleep. Just about that same moment, the angel of the Lord Gabriel appeared to him in a dream.

The angel said, "Joseph, thou son of David, fear not to take unto thee Mary, as thy wife: for that which is conceived in her is of the Holy Ghost. She shall bring forth a son, and thou shalt call his name Jesus; for He shall save His people from their sins." He also reminded Joseph that it was written by the prophet, Isaiah, about the virgin having a man-child and His name being called Immanuel, which being interpreted is "God with us."

Then Joseph awakened from sleep and did as the angel of the Lord had bidden him, and he got up, dressed, and ran to my house to tell me the news. Later that day, we were married. Our marriage ceremony was not fancy, and there was no big wedding feast afterward, but I was just happy to have Joseph, and especially to have him know that I was telling him the truth of the Holy Conception. I knew that God had blessed our marriage and now we were patiently awaiting the birth of Jesus, the Son of God!

No one had any way of knowing that I had become pregnant before Joseph and I were married. However, some of the women would seemingly shun me to a point. At times, I would hear the older women whisper about me at the well; that is if they would even get water at the same time as I did. Usually, the women would see me standing at the well and act as if they had forgotten something and turn the other way. No one said anything to me, but I knew they silently judged me because they weren't friendly toward me anymore. Most of them would not even speak to me when they passed me.

No one was going to believe that there had been a virginal holy conception, or that the angel of the Lord had appeared to both me and Joseph, or that the child I was carrying was from the Heavenly Father—God Himself. I didn't try to explain anything to them because I knew that everything was in God's hands. I would just put my hand on my stomach and say, "Father, forgive them." Little did I know that my baby would say the same words, as He gave his life on the cruel cross of Calvary for the sins of the world, some thirty-three years later.

I knew that Joseph knew the truth and Father God was the only one who could rightfully judge me, and I found comfort in the love of an Almighty God. As the days passed, nothing else mattered except doing everything that the Lord God had commanded us to do. At times, I felt unworthy, but I knew that I was truly blessed among women. I would strive to be the best mother and the God-fearing woman I was meant to be. After realizing my blessing, I wholeheartedly accepted the calling that God himself had given me.

Joseph was so patient and loving; neither of us could wait for the birth of Jesus. We would lie awake, all hours of the night discussing the angel's visit and the Blessed Event headed our way. We spoke of how much we loved our Lord and would pray deep into the night, both thanking Him for choosing us, and we were asking Him to help us to be able to righteously honor the Gift that He had bestowed upon us. When Joseph got up at daybreak to go to the carpenter shop; he wasn't even tired.

I kept busy doing daily chores of cleaning around the house and washing clothes and the days seemed to pass rather quickly. Early some mornings, before the sun would come up and the day would be hot, I would get up, get dressed, and take a short walk down by the little brook where I went to wash clothes. At that time of the morning, it would be just warm enough outside to be comfortable, and I would sit on the bank, watching the clear, cool water flowing and think about how much that my life had changed in the past few months. I just wanted to be a good mother to my precious baby boy. The weather always seemed to be nice, and since it didn't rain very often, I could go walking at least two or three days a week.

One beautiful sunshiny morning, while I was out walking, I began to think about my sweet cousin and best friend, Elizabeth. I decided that I would love to go and visit with her and stay a few days. I knew that she was about six months along in her pregnancy. I just needed to spend some time with another woman who knew exactly how I was feeling. She, too, was carrying a miracle from God.

Later that afternoon, when Joseph came home from work, I told him that I would love to visit her for a few days. He said that he thought that was a very good idea and that our spending a little time together would be good medicine for both of us. As he was helping me pack my clothes for the trip, I remember thinking, *My husband must be the greatest and most caring man in the entire world.* The next morning, Joseph walked with me to the home of Elizabeth and Zacharias.

My few days' visit lasted about three months. Joseph would come over for dinner a few evenings each week, and he and Zacharias would walk and talk awhile and then he would leave early to go home so he could get a little rest before going to work the next day. Although I missed him very much, I still enjoyed the memorable time that Elizabeth and I spent together.

Chapter 2

Unto You a "Savior"

Elizabeth and Zacharias had been promised a son in their youth, but now they were growing old. At her age, for Elizabeth to conceive a child would be a miracle. A child would not only be an answered prayer for them from many years past, but most of all, it would be God's promise fulfilled.

She and I spent a lot of time together during our pregnancies. We would sit and talk for hours about our sons, and how the angel Gabriel had appeared to both of us. I remember when I first saw her, while we were hugging hello, she smiled and said that the baby inside her was leaping for joy because he knew that the child I was carrying was the Son of God!

Now the angel Gabriel had also appeared to Elizabeth's husband, Zacharias, and had told him that Elizabeth was going to bear a son. He began to laugh and he said, "My wife is much too old to have a child and I do not believe that this thing you speak of could possibly happen." The angel became angry at his nonbelief and said to him, "Because you do not believe and trust God to answer your prayers in His time, you shall become dumb and not be allowed to speak a word until the birth of the baby, whom God has said, you must call him by the name John." From that moment until the baby John was born, Zacharias's only communication was to either grunt and point or to write his words on a writing table. Occasionally, his not being able to talk became frustrating for him and he would get angry; but then he would stop, smile, and looking toward the sky, mouth the words, "Please forgive me!" and "Thank you" and picking up his table, he would begin to write the words that he wanted to say.

I spent the last month of Elizabeth's pregnancy with her. I helped her with her chores, and sometimes we would find an old robe or piece of cloth, tear it, and sew garments and hats for the babies. One of the ladies in the village had given her a remnant of lamb's wool, and she cut it in half and gave one of the pieces to me. We happily made each of the babies a soft cloak. It was only then that we realized just how small our babies would be at birth.

Then early one evening, Elizabeth began to sweat profusely, and she was having pains in her lower back. They grew very harsh, and she had paced back and forth across the room until she had become so tired that she had to lie down. A few hours later, she had a short but very painful delivery.

Zacharias was beside himself; he was so excited and blessed, but as he paced the floor, during the time of her labor, we could see that his heart was hurting. He seemed to be feeling the pain and suffering along with his beloved wife. He could not speak, but he moaned along with her. He even had tears building up in his eyes.

As the baby was born, the presence of God filled the entire room. Praise and glory went up to God from everywhere. Dear Elizabeth fell into a much-needed peaceful sleep. The woman who was helping her with the delivery covered the baby with a small towel and handed him to his father who was smiling with pride. Zacharias held the baby in one hand and raised his other hand up to God in praise.

On the eighth day after the baby was born, Zacharias could speak for the first time since he had been struck dumb by the angel Gabriel because of his nonbelief. He then proclaimed the baby boy's name to be John. Both he and Elizabeth, their faces shinning with a heavenly glow, lifted their hands up toward heaven and gave God all the praise and glory for the blessing that He had given to them.

BLESSED AMONG WOMEN

The following morning, I decided that it was time to return to Joseph and my family. It would only be three months until I was to deliver my precious little Baby Boy, the true Son of God! I hugged Elizabeth, patted the baby's hand, picked up my travel bag, and started out the door. Looking down the road, I saw Joseph coming to bring me home. It was a long walk to our home, and he was afraid that it would not be safe for me to walk so far alone in my condition, as he always lovingly called my pregnancy.

Days turned into weeks and then, about the time I was to deliver, a decree went out from Caesar Augustus, the emperor of Rome, that all the world would be taxed. At the time, Caesar was the ruler of the world.

Everyone had to go into the city of his birth. Joseph and I had to go from Galilee, out of Nazareth, into Judea, and on to Bethlehem, to be counted and to pay our taxes. Because Joseph was of the lineage of David, he had to go to Bethlehem, which is known throughout all of Israel and to all the Jewish people as the city of David.

About the middle of the next week, early in the evening, Joseph came in from a long, hard day's work in the carpenter shop. He said that we must leave at dawn the next morning to make our long hard journey to Bethlehem. The city of Bethlehem would be about seventy-five miles or 125 kilometers away.

I couldn't bring myself to tell Joseph that I had been feeling bad all day and had been having light pains in the lower part of back. God had brought us this far; He would see us all the way. I didn't want to remind him that my delivery time was drawing near. I knew that I had to go with him and I also knew that the tiresome journey would take a few days because we would have to stop often to rest. There was no doubt in my mind that the baby would be born before we could return to Nazareth. He would probably be born in or near the city of Bethlehem.

I quickly prepared for the long journey. I baked a few little cakes of bread and put some honey in a sack for our meals. Joseph filled three gourds with water. We packed a couple of blankets and some strips of cloth for the baby. After we had finished getting everything ready for the journey, we decided to try to get some sleep because it would not be long until dawn. Joseph knew that the long trip ahead would be a hard one for a man and his expectant wife who was due to deliver her baby at any time now. I am sure that he dreaded it almost as much as I did, if not more.

I rode our sweet little donkey. Although the ride was rough and at times even a little painful, I was still thankful to God that I didn't have to walk such a long distance. The journey was indeed long and very tiring. Joseph stopped frequently for me to rest. He made sure that I drank a lot of water on the trip. I didn't think that we were ever going to get to Bethlehem. I longed for a good bath and a nice, comfortable bed and a good night's sleep. I would ride a short distance, and then the pains in my back would start again, and I would have to ask Joseph to stop, often we had just gotten started.

I hated to slow him down, but he had known from the beginning that the trip was going to be long and hard for both of us. I didn't tell him, but I was so afraid the baby would be born along the way. I realize now that he probably had the same fear that the baby would be delivered before we reached Bethlehem as I did, and I could see from the expressions on his face that he felt every pain and discomfort that I had.

The donkey was so sweet and so careful not to stumble, and she stepped ever so softly on the rough, rocky road. I remember telling Joseph that this animal could have been shown by the Spirit of the Lord that she was carrying the Son of God and His earthly mother.

The weather was very good throughout the journey. The noon sun did not get unbearably hot, and in the evening, when we stopped to make our camp for the night, the wind was very still and the nights were just warm enough to be comfortable.

Finally, after four long days and nights, we were almost to the end of our journey. We found refuge in a large rocky cave. We had stopped early to make our camp for the night so we could get some much-needed rest before reaching the city. There was a long, wide ledge along the back wall. It was just wide enough and long enough for both of us to make a nice bed. When we spread out our blankets, the ledge became very comfortable.

We were almost out of food, and we only had a couple of little cakes left that I had packed. I told Joseph to eat them both because I was just too tired to eat. However, he insisted that I must not go to bed with an empty stomach. As we ate, we sat and talked for a little while. We both knew that the baby would be born in Bethlehem, and we were both excited and a little scared. We finally decided to get some sleep.

Knowing that the delivery was so near, I didn't get much sleep, because I kept thinking about the baby. Like any new mother expecting her first child, I had so many questions. I was wondering how He would look. I had not been around a lot of babies, and all of them do not have a head full of hair. I already loved Him so much that I didn't care if he had hair; I only hoped that I could make Him happy and He would not cry a lot. I just wanted to be a good mother to Him. I was becoming nervous about raising God's Son. He had trusted me with a very special blessing, and I only wanted to please HIM. Finally, I asked HIM just to lead me and guide me the way HE wanted me to go and then I turned toward the wall and fell into a deep, restful sleep.

Joseph was up long before I was awake. He was quietly getting something ready for us for breakfast, and he was letting me sleep a little longer because he knew that I was exhausted. The warm sunshine finally had begun to shine into the opening of the cave and made me open my eyes.

"Good morning! I was beginning to wonder if you were going to sleep the whole day!" Joseph chuckled as he planted a soft kiss on my cheek.

"Good morning to you too," I said, smiling. "I feel so refreshed and rested that I am ready to go to Bethlehem. Oh, what are you doing?"

He said, "I'm trying to fix a quick bite for us to eat. Some travelers passed a little while ago, and I bought two doves and a couple of cakes of bread from them. They said that we still have about a half day's journey left. We should reach Bethlehem before sunset, even having to stop several times to rest!"

Finally, we saw Bethlehem in the distance. It was the most beautiful sight that I had ever seen. I couldn't wait to get there, and I was so happy as we came into the city. I just couldn't wait to get a nice room in one of the inns and to be able to wash the dust of the journey from my body before giving birth to the precious baby I was carrying. I could feel myself becoming very tired and weak.

To our dismay, we found the entire city to be very crowded. Everyone was running to and fro. There was a lot of loud talking and laughing, bargaining for goods, and a lot pushing and shoving. It seemed that no one had any concern for anyone but himself. There were hundreds of people everywhere as far as your eyes could see; I had never seen so many people in one place.

Joseph said that we would find a nice place to stay for the night, and then he would quickly feed and water the little donkey. After he had everything settled for the evening, we could find ourselves something to eat and then lie down and get some very much needed rest. We went from inn to inn, seeking a room for the night just to be turned away because they were all filled. Some had two, three, and even four families to a room. We stopped at the last inn in the city and had given up hope of finding any lodging or shelter. As we turned to leave, the innkeeper called to Joseph.

"Sir, I know this may sound terrible, but I do have a clean stable around behind the inn. You and your wife are welcome to stay in there and take shelter in a nice soft bed of straw. She looks so very tired and almost ready to deliver her child."

Now I was thinking, to bring forth a newborn baby in a dirty, smelly stable with animals making all kinds of noises, how could that be? The Son of God born here! I knew that God would provide so I would be happy to bed down for the night and get some rest. To my surprise, we found the stable to be very neat and clean, even sweet smelling. The smell of the animals was not at all noticeable. I was right, God Himself did provide what He wanted for His Son.

Joseph took the fresh, clean straw and made me a very comfortable bed over near the back wall and next to a little manger. Then he said, "Look, Mary, we can put some of this straw in the manger and make a cozy little bed for the baby when He arrives."

Neither of us was hungry, so after Joseph had fed and watered the little donkey, we just decided to get some rest and wait until morning to eat. As I lay there trying to get to sleep, I began to think about the past few months of my pregnancy.

I would lie awake at night after I had begun to feel the baby moving, and I would touch my stomach and feel the sweetness and goodness and the glory of GOD. I felt as if I were living in a beautiful dream and I expected to awaken at any moment.

I tried to imagine the sound of His voice. I wondered how the Son of God would act as He grew into a man. So many questions were in my mind. I just wanted to be the mother that God wanted me to be.

Suddenly, the pain was becoming almost unbearable. I knew the time was very near. I called to Joseph who had just fallen asleep and told him that I thought the time had come. Joseph held tightly to my hand, and we just waited until the child was born. Seeing a small well located out next to the rear of the little stable, Joseph had filled our gourds with water. We tried to wash and clean the baby up as best we could. I wrapped Him in the little strips of cloth that I had brought and then handed Him to Joseph, who gently laid him in the little manger.

The presence of God filled the stable. The animals seemed to be singing a lullaby so soft and low that the wind made the music. As I placed a kiss on my newborn son's forehead, I knew that I, Mary, who was blessed among women, had just kissed the face of the Son of God!

Joseph and I both bowed on our knees and gave thanks and praise to the Lord and His Son! Still, as an earthly mother who had just given birth, I knew in my heart from that moment on that HE was indeed the "*Savior*" of the world! The three of us fell into a peaceful sleep.

We were awakened in the middle of the night by a small band of shepherds who had been watching over their flocks in the fields just a short distance from Bethlehem. The elder-shepherd began to tell us his story of how they came to find the newborn child.

He said, "We were abiding in our fields keeping watch over our sheep, and lo, the angel of the Lord came upon us, and glory of the Lord shone round us, and we were sore afraid. Then the angel said unto us, 'Fear not, for, behold, I bring you good tidings of great joy, which shall be to all people. For unto you is born this day in the city of David a Savior, which is Christ the Lord; and this shall be a sign unto you, ye shall find the Babe wrapped in swaddling clothes and lying in a manger.' And suddenly there was with the angel a multitude of the heavenly host praising God and saying, 'Glory to God in the highest, and on earth peace, and good-will toward men.' After the angels had left, we decided to come to Bethlehem to see this thing which has come to pass, which the Lord has made known to us. We were guided by a huge bright heavenly star. May we, please see this Child?"

Joseph handed me the Baby, and the shepherds looked at Him and then fell on their knees and worshiped Him. They didn't stay but just a few minutes because the elder-shepherd told them that I must be very tired. With a slight bow and a nod, one by one they left to go to their flocks while praising and glorifying GOD.

Joseph said, "Mary, it is written in the days of old by the prophet, Isaiah, that a virgin shall conceive and bear a Son and call His name Immanuel! How blessed I am to be the husband of that virgin. Glory to God! Our Lord has trusted us with His most valuable possession in all of Heaven, His Only Begotten Son."

Again, Joseph and I decided to try to get a little rest before daybreak. We tucked the baby nice and snug back into His bed in the manger and then laid down ourselves for a little sleep.

The next morning, Joseph found us a small cottage behind one of the inns. We had to stay a few weeks until we could perform all the required duties of new parents according to our custom for firstborn male children. After forty days, we should be able to return to our home in Nazareth.

The first week of being a mother was a little trying at times. I was so scared that I would do something wrong, and I seemed to be tired so often. Joseph would help me as much as he could, and finally, after about a week, I had rested enough and felt more like myself again. I was becoming very comfortable looking after this precious baby. I was truly a mother now and what a very Special Child I had!

Chapter 3

The Dedication of the Lamb

It was Jewish custom that when a baby boy became eight days old, he must be circumcised. Just after the circumcision, Joseph, doing as the angel Gabriel had told him, declared the baby's name to be Jesus. Also, it was Jewish custom that when the firstborn male child became forty days old, he was to be taken to the temple and to be dedicated to God. We took Jesus to the temple in Jerusalem for His dedication.

The mother of the child was to take two unblemished turtledoves to present as a sacrifice to the Lord. One was to be offered as a sin offering, and the other one was to be offered as a burnt offering.

At first, when we arrived at the temple, we didn't see or hear anyone. As we walked to the door and not hearing any movement inside, we thought that we would more than likely have to leave and return later that day. Starting to depart through the side door, we saw an elderly man walking toward us. When he was close enough to speak, he introduced himself, and he said that his name was Simeon.

After talking with him for a few minutes, we realized that he was a just and devout man who God loved very much. He was waiting for the consolation of Israel. The Holy Ghost had revealed to him that he would not see death before he had seen the Lord's Christ.

We also learned that at the same time Joseph and I had taken Jesus to the temple, the Holy Spirit had lead Simeon there just ahead of us. I didn't know why at the time, but I felt comfortable enough to hand my newborn Baby Jesus to this man, whom I had just met. There was a sweet spirit about him, and we were all rejoicing in the Lord!

Simeon took Jesus in his arms and holding Him up to GOD said these exact words,

"Lord, now let Thou thy servant depart in peace, according to thy word: For mine eyes have seen thy salvation, which thou hast prepared before the face of all people; A light to lighten the Gentiles, and the Glory of Thy people, Israel."

Joseph and I were amazed at those things that Simeon spoke about the Baby Jesus. We knew that he had to have been shown by the Holy Spirit that Jesus was indeed the Christ. Then he blessed us and turning to me, he said, "Behold this Child is set for the fall and rising again of many in Israel; and for a sign which shall be spoken against; (yea, a sword shall pierce through thy soul also.) that the thoughts of many hearts may be revealed."

At that time, I did not understand everything that Simeon was telling me. I had no idea the suffering and shame that Jesus as a man would come to endure. I had no idea the suffering, as a mother, I too would know, as I watch my son being tortured and seeing him die on the cruel cross of Calvary some thirty-three years later. The cross that my son would bear for the entire human race, both Jew and Gentile alike.

Then the priest came into the room and, taking the baby from Joseph, held Him up before the altar and inscribed the name "Jesus" on the roll of the firstborn. He did not recognize the Baby for who He was. He was holding the "True High Priest" in his hands, the actual "King of Glory," the "Infant Redeemer!"

And when all the things were performed according to the law of the Lord, we left the temple and decided to begin our journey back to Galilee to our home in Nazareth. We were so excited for everyone, all our friends and family to meet our newborn son. We had planned to leave very early the next morning.

However, as we had walked a short distance down the path, we met a man, who told us that his name was James. He said that he wanted to restore an old inn that he had bought. It was located a couple of miles out of town and needed some new furniture to get it started. He said that all the furniture that had been left in the building was badly worn, and many new pieces would be needed. The long list included a few tables, several chairs, and some tall hanging closets. James said that he had been told by some of the men in the area that Joseph was a carpenter by trade.

Explaining that if Joseph would consider staying in Jerusalem for a while longer and making the furniture for him, that he had a cottage with a small shed behind it at the back of the inn and offered to let us live in it, rent free, while he was building the furniture.

Joseph accepted the job, and we moved into the house. The shed became the ideal place for his carpenter shop. It was already well stocked with many tools, and all Joseph had to do was to get started. The request for the new furniture was a Blessing because it would provide us with a little extra money to take back to Nazareth for our new home. We needed to add some more space now that we had a new son to raise. We had spent all our extra money on food and provisions just after the baby was born.

We were very happy in our new home. It was nice and cozy. There was a large stream right out from the back door that provided us with plenty of water for cooking, bathing, and washing clothes and two large fruit trees in the front yard. Out behind the house were grapevines hanging full of big, beautiful purple grapes and James said that my having a small vegetable garden in the yard near the fruit trees was a splendid idea.

There was plenty to eat, and everything that we could need was right there, because, as always, God did provide.

Joseph's work went very well, and James was overjoyed with the beautiful furniture. Almost every day, he would stop by the shed and add something else that he wanted Joseph to make, to his already long list of needed pieces. He kept having his men bring in more and more lumber. Joseph didn't mind because not only did he enjoy carpentry, but it also meant a lot more money than we had expected for us to take home and besides adding more room to our home, we were overjoyed because we could also help some of our family with their financial needs.

Baby Jesus was growing so fast. He could sit up in the floor by himself, for long periods of time and to play with the donkey, lamb, and other toys that Joseph had crafted for Him from small scraps of lumber. He was a very happy little fellow, and He always had a sweet loving smile for everyone.

One beautiful afternoon, I was sitting out in the yard under a big shade tree, holding Jesus, trying to teach Him to patty cake, putting His little hands together and playing and singing with Him. He had just awakened from a long nap and was feeling ready to play. The wife of the man who owned the cottage that we were living in was taking an evening walk and just as she started to pass the house, she heard the Baby's laughter. Looking over toward the big tree, she saw us sitting there and walked over to us. We introduced ourselves and just started talking. She was an older lady who said that her name was Anna.

There was an extra chair leaning against the tree, so I invited her to sit with us for a while. As we were talking, she said that she was unable to have children and she loved them so much. We found that we had so much in common, and it seemed as if we had known each other forever. After we had talked a few minutes, Anna, looking so lovingly toward Jesus, smiled and asked me if she could hold my beautiful baby. I handed Jesus to her and from the first moment that she held Him, she began to love Him so much, and He loved her as if she were His grandmother. After that day, she would often stop in to visit with us late in the afternoon just to play with the baby for a while.

It was she, not I, who had taught Him to clap His little hands and to wave goodbye. The two of us became very good friends, and we love just to sit and talk with each other. Sometimes, I would trade her the extra vegetables from my garden for a new recipe to try that night for dinner. Once or twice a week, she and her husband James would come to visit and the four of us would eat dinner together. Then we would go out and sit in the shade of the big trees and talk late into the evening until it was time for them to go home for the night.

I knew that when it came time for us to return to Nazareth that we would truly miss their friendship very much because Anna and James had become very dear friends to both Joseph and me. We knew that soon we would have to leave them and go home to our friends and family in Nazareth. A few years later, when we were finally settled at home, we learned that we would never see James and Anna again.

Sadly, we heard that Anna had died from some heart ailment, only a short time after we had left. A couple of months later, James had been bitten by a poisonous snake, a viper, while fishing with some of his kinsmen near the Sea of Galilee and had died instantly.

There is an appointed time for all of us humans who are living on the earth to die, but it is a very lonely time for our loved ones whom we leave behind.

Chapter 4

The Flight into Egypt

Jesus was a young child, less than two years old, and we had not yet returned to our home country of Nazareth. One evening, right after sunset, just barely dark, we were visited by wise men (astrologers) from the East who said that they had been following a large, bright star for about two years. It had led them to this house, and they were looking for the Christ Child and wanted to worship Him. The men believed Him to be the Messiah prophesied by Isaiah, the prophet, because of the "guiding star" and that He had been born to become the "King of the Jews." They brought him gifts of gold, frankincense, and myrrh. (I kept them in a little wooden box until He was grown.) The wise men bowed down and worshiped him, and again the Glory of God covered the room. God had shown them in their hearts that Jesus was, indeed, the Christ whom they were seeking.

The Wise Men told us that they had stopped at the palace in Jerusalem and talked with King Herod about the "guiding star." They told him that they had been following it for almost two years and they had finally seen it come to a stop around about over Bethlehem. They also told him of the prophecy of the new King of Israel and everything that was written about Him by Prophet Isaiah. Herod was very interested in the young child and had asked them on their return to please stop at the palace and give him the exact location and His name so he that could also come and worship the "Child Messiah."

We did not know at the time, but when the men left, God had shown them in their hearts that Herod was playing a deceitful, evil trick and was planning to kill Him. The men took much longer route home and never returned to Herod because they feared for the Child's life.

That same night, the Angel of the Lord, Gabriel, again appeared to Joseph in a dream. He told him to arise quickly and to take Jesus to Egypt where He would be safe because there were some very evil men who were planning to kill Him. We jumped up out of bed in the middle of the night and, as fast as we could, grabbed a couple of blankets, packed a few clothes, some food, and the little money that we had saved and silently left out before daybreak. We were very careful, making certain that no one saw us leaving or would have any idea of the direction that we had taken.

When we reached Egypt, it was easy to find a place to settle in until the Lord God told us what would be our next move. Again, we found a makeshift dwelling and Joseph acquired odd carpentry jobs to make our living as we patiently awaited the Will of the Lord. We knew that we were nestled safely in His protection and that He would provide us with everything that we needed.

We learned somewhat later that King Herod, who was the wicked king of Judaea, had inquired of the wisest men in his kingdom, about the prophecy of Isaiah concerning a King who was to rule Israel. He would come out of Bethlehem of Judaea, and Herod greatly feared that Jesus was that "King." He decided to find the Christ Child and kill him. The prophesy had frightened the scribes, the priests, and all the other mighty men of Jerusalem because they feared that if the Christ Child was the "One" of whom Isaiah was referring, that when word got out, there would be chaos over the entire land. They feared that the Romans would be killing everyone, particularly the Jews.

Herod became even more terrified and very angry when he had realized that the astrologers from the East did not return to him with the news of the new possible King of the Jews. He said that they had betrayed him and had made a fool of him. He again consulted the wisest men in his kingdom to meet with him at the palace to help him to devise a plan to stop this nonsense before if it had gone any farther.

Every one of them advised him that he must have the Christ Child killed. Now having no way of being sure that he would get the Christ Child because he didn't know exactly where to find Him, King Herod decided to send some of his soldiers to Bethlehem and even throughout the coastal area. He had ordered them to slaughter the male children who were two years old and younger, even the newborns were to be killed. We were told that the heartless soldiers grabbed some of the baby boys right out of their mother's arms and ran their swords through them. The poor mothers could do nothing but beg for their baby's lives, as they had cried and screamed for them to stop. Many of the soldiers had become angry and killed them as well. After the slaughter of the firstborn males of the House of Israel, the soldiers were certain that the Christ Child had been killed. They returned to the king and told him that He was indeed dead because they had not left one baby boy alive in the whole country side. Having no idea of the protection that the Heavenly Father had provided "His Son" that very night, Herod thought that his cruel, evil deed would not only teach the Jews a lesson, but at the same time would eliminate all chances of a new king taking his throne. After all, the mass slaughter had taken place and everyone would have been too afraid of the soldiers to have let any baby boy escape his fate. Herod said that neighbor would turn against neighbor to save his own life and the lives of the rest of his family.

Early one morning, Joseph woke me up and said, "Mary, you can start packing, we can go back home now. The Angel of the Lord Gabriel visited me last night in a dream and told me that we could arise and return to Israel because King Herod and all the men who wished to do harm to Jesus are dead."

When we came into the land of Israel, we learned that Herod's evil son, Archelaus, now reigned in his father Herod's place and because Joseph had been warned in his heart again, we turned aside into Galilee, in the city of Nazareth just as it is written by the prophet. "HE shall be called a Nazarene!"

We felt that we had come "home" for a while. Joseph set up his carpenter shop and began working, and we got everything settled in our new home. Young Jesus kept growing both spiritually and physically. His precious smile would light up the entire room, and He smiled all the time. By now, He was beginning to carry on a conversation with everyone, and His little voice was very soft and sweet.

Joseph loved Him so much, and every afternoon when he came home from work, and we had eaten our evening meal, about an hour or so before bedtime, the two of them would sit and talk. They would start wrestling with each other until it was time to lie down. They always laughed and giggled and had so much fun. I would laugh at them as they played. We always had such a joyful time together. Jesus would begin to get tired, start rubbing His eyes, as all little children do when they become sleepy, and then the three of us would kneel together, have our evening prayer, and immediately afterward, Joseph and I would put Him to bed. Every night, He always had to give both of us a big bear hug, as He called it, and kiss on the cheek before He could go to sleep.

Chapter 5

Memories of the Child Jesus

For the most part, Jesus was a child just like any other "human" child in that His needs were the same as theirs. He needed food, water, shelter, guidance, and most of all unconditional love and understanding.

I would say that it would be almost impossible for the human mind to imagine that the Infant Jesus had feelings just like any other "human" baby has. He soiled His clothes, had His gums hurt while He was cutting His teeth. He had stomachaches, would sometimes become nauseous and spit up, and He did a million other things, just like all babies do—let me tell you, He sure did!

It must be impossible for the human mind to imagine that Jesus as a little boy was also, a lot like any other "human" boy. He was mischievous, laughed, giggled, and even at times, would wipe His runny nose on His sleeve. He had colds, headaches, and would perspire when playing outside in the heat of the day and would get chills and freeze when winter time came. He romped, ran, and played with the other boys of the village.

All the boys in the village would climb the big shade trees in the side yard and jump off a high limb and land on the ground. None of Jesus's bones were ever broken, and I don't think that John had any broken bones, but I seem to remember that he sprained his ankle one summer. Another one of the boys had broken his wrist one evening while they were all climbing the trees.

Jesus had loose teeth and often stumped his toes, got heartbroken, and cried, and He would get tired and need to rest, and He did a million other things, just like all little "human" boys do, but let me tell you, He sure did.

He was happy all the time and had no temper at all, and He loved everybody with unconditional love. There were many differences, yet there were many similarities too.

Yes, throughout the short life that He lived on earth, Jesus experienced many of the feelings that every other human on earth would experience. After He grew into manhood, He had so many emotional heartaches such as the betrayal of a friend, the death of some of his loved ones, and witnessing the abuse of many people as well as animals. He also had to experience pain, agony, frustration, and confusion. I am sure that the worst heartache of all for Him was the extreme evil of a deceitful and hate filled human race for which He had left His throne in Glory to come to save. He was God in the flesh, but He did not make a perfect life on earth for Himself, although He could have. He wanted to live as a man and endure the hardships that the people whom He loved so much, sometimes had to face.

There are so many memorial moments of Jesus as a child, but one of my fondest memories of Jesus as a baby is the pure love that I felt when He would nestle as close as He could get to my heart and sleep for hours. It was as if my heartbeat put Him to sleep. He always had a sweet smile on His face. I knew that He would only be with me for a short time because He was here to serve His Father. But He was still my "son," and being so young at the time, I did not understand everything at once. God only revealed a little bit at a time, only what He knew that my human brain could comprehend and in "His own good time" of course.

Knowing that the road ahead was going to be long and hard, but at the same time, having no idea of the suffering and heartache that we were going to go through, I felt it to be worth it all. Every time that I looked into the face of my son, my Lord and my God, and every time that I planted a kiss on his precious little cheek or gave him a hug, I knew that I was "Blessed among Woman." When Jesus was very young, maybe three or four, he could already read so well. Joseph and I would school him, and we would read to Him from the Scriptures together. Having an amazing memory, He could always remember everything that we had read. He had an understanding that was so far advanced, even as a very young child, and would sometimes explain passages to Joseph and me and to anyone else who might ask Him. Of course, we both knew that His knowledge came from the Heavenly Father.

He and John would play together and discuss the prophets of old. They would talk about Moses and Abraham. Jesus acted as though He had walked with them and now after everything has come to pass, I realize that He did.

Another time, He and John were running and playing some sort of game with some other children. He and John and another one of the boys slipped and fell in some rocks. John and the boy were both bleeding. They had cuts and scratches on their knees and elbows, but Jesus only had a few scratches and some dirt on his knees. He wasn't bleeding at all, not one drop of blood.

No one even seemed to notice. (I am sure that God kept everyone's mind on John and the little boy and their injuries.) We did not realize at the time that the "Blood of Jesus" was being preserved by His Holy Father to wash away the sins of the world. I took Him inside and wiped the dirt and grime from His knees and sent Him back outside to play with His two little friends.

One spring day, when Jesus was probably about six years old, He was outside playing near the far corner of our house. Suddenly a small white dove flew into the side of the house and hitting the wall, broke its neck and fell with a thud to the ground. He ran over to it, picked it up ever so gently, and still holding it in His sweet little hands, began to cry so hard that His tears were soaking the bird's feathers.

"Oh, how sad, Mother," He cried. It is so important to the Father!" He then kissed the dove and held it in His hands up to God. The baby dove started to move, it turned over and over, lifted its head, and stood up in Jesus's hands, and as He opened them, it flew away cooing. Glory was all around us! Jesus fell on His knees and gave thanks to God for saving the dove's life.

He loved animals, and they all seemed to love Him. I have seen them praise His name many times. At His birth and even as He was lying in the manger, all the animals in the barn softly sang Him to sleep. It has been such a blessing from God to see His Son grow into a man and the biggest blessing of all was that He had allowed him to be "my son" for a short time as He walked on the earth. I learned very early that blessings come hand in hand with suffering and they help us to bare our pain! Shortly after Jesus was born, I realized what a blessing that Father God had given me.

I have seen Jesus as a very young boy teaching many times in the Temple, on the banks of the river, out in the fields, and down at the marketplace, where the people would bring their goods to sell. Sometimes when we would take long walks, I have even known some of the older men to stop and ask his opinion on many important matters. When they would finish talking, the men would walk away amazed at the understanding the young child had and the helpful advice that He was able to give them.

Jesus always obeyed the Laws of Moses and, even as a child, honored His earthly mother and father. Never raising His voice for any reason, He was always soft-hearted, loving, very well-mannered, and so sweet tempered. He learned quickly, and the scriptures were where He excelled the most.

I also remember when Jesus was just a young boy and our donkey had given birth a few weeks early, the baby donkey was already dead when it was born. It had the umbilical cord wrapped around its neck. Jesus went to unwrap the cord and lay facedown on the baby donkey's side. With tears running from his eyes, He began silently praying and rubbing the donkey's face. Suddenly the little donkey raised its head and Jesus moved back. The donkey that we had planned to call Precious began to bray softly, then it sat up and in a few minutes was standing by its mother's side. She had seemed to be smiling at her new baby, and she was softly breathing as she began cleaning it, licking it so lovingly. Both Jesus and I raised our hands toward heaven, giving praise and glory to God! I thought I could hear harps ringing softly in the distance.

Jesus was never still. He was always busy, either playing with His lambs or some of His friends or studying the scriptures. One of His baby lambs got its foot caught in a thorn bush. When it had finally wiggled itself free, its leg was cut really bad and bleeding. Jesus broke a piece of aloe plant and smoothed the juice on its cuts, wrapped its leg in a small clean cloth, and began rocking the injured lamb in His arms. Rubbing its side, He began softly humming and it went to sleep, just like a human baby would do. He held it the rest of the day until bedtime. Joseph took it to the shed and laid it beside its mother. The next morning, the little lamb was scampering around playing with Jesus and the other children, acting as if it had never been hurt.

Jesus had fed the hungry from the time that He was old enough to walk around the neighborhood by himself, probably at the age of seven or eight. As a child, He made friends easily with both children and adults. He saw no age, color, or religious differences and He loved everyone.

An elderly man would come into the marketplace every morning walking very slowly with the aid of a cane. He would sit in the middle of the square and beg alms from the people who would pass His way. He had fallen and broken his right leg as a young man, and it didn't heal properly, causing him to remain a cripple for the rest of his life, also he had been blind in his left eye from birth. Jesus saw him sitting and leaning up against a tree late one evening, begging for money that he said he needed to buy bread for him and his wife and daughter. He thought that the man might be hungry because he had been sitting there most of the day. At the time, Jesus was eating a honey cake and had a small bottle of water.

He broke off the piece of cake where he had just taken a bite and walked over to the man and introduced Himself and the man told him that his name was Simon. Jesus handed the cake to the man and then gave him a drink from His water bottle. The man was so grateful to Him. He just kept smiling, and then with a tearful eye, he sat there eating the cake. Jesus would become heartbroken anytime that He thought that anyone might be hungry, especially an elderly person or a young child.

He was always willing to help with anything that Joseph or I needed to be done. He would even help the neighbor families with their work on occasion. One thing that He would do every evening, just before sunset, was to go to the well and to carry a bucket of water for the elderly lady, Hannah. She lived down the road a short way. Jesus did not want her to have to go to the well and get it by herself. She was a widow woman and had no children of her own or any family to help her. He feared that she might fall and be severely injured. He had so much love for His fellow man and was ready at any moment to lend a hand or to offer a word of encouragement when He felt it was needed.

Even as a young child, His ability to help people solve their problems was amazing. His voice was always so soft, and His eyes were full of love and compassion. As a man, many years later while hanging on the cross, He looked out into the huge crowd and asked His Father in heaven. "Please forgive them because they knew not what they do!"

Another special memory I have of His life with me is that He was very fond of Joseph, His "earthly father." When He was still a child, maybe even ten or eleven years old, he insisted that He must help Joseph in the carpenter shop almost every day. Many nights, the two of them would come home from a long hard day and were so exhausted that as soon as they could get a quick bite to eat, they would fall into bed. They would get up the next morning to begin another long day. Jesus never once grumbled or complained about anything or even mentioned being the least bit tired.

Always laughing and very mischievous, He loved to tease Joseph and me by hiding our sandals behind a chair or under our bed. Many mornings, He would awaken us with the same little "wake up song" that he had sung the morning after we had returned from Jerusalem for the Passover.

All the years of His life, while I was blessed to be "His mother," I loved Him with all my heart as an earthly mother loves her son, but I also loved Him as a woman loves her Lord! I could feel my heart swell with pride and love each time He would say, "I love you, Mother Mary." It was always followed by a big hug and a kiss on the cheek.

Jesus was growing stronger and getting taller every day. When He was almost twelve years old, he was already a couple of inches taller than me. He was known throughout our village as the tall, skinny son of Joseph, the carpenter. We would tease Him and call Him our big, little giant and He would just laugh. As a child, He never became angry at anyone or anything; except when He had seen bullying or abuse, he would become upset with the person, who He thought to be hurting another. He always played well with all the children of the village. When they would gather at our home, we never heard any of them having a cross word with each other. They all played so well together.

When He and John were in their early teenage years, they became very good fishermen, and we would have fish almost every day for either our noon or evening meal. Sometimes they caught enough fish to supply both of our families an entire meal and have enough left to share with the neighbors.

Speaking of sharing, all the people of the village would willingly share their food, water, firewood, clothing, and when needed, were also willing to share some of their time to help each other. Both Jesus and John could always be found, right in the middle of the crowd wanting and ready to do anything they could to help.

The boys were quickly growing into men and both Elizabeth and I knew that very soon, our sons would leave our homes and began doing the Will of God! Being blessed throughout our lives while our sons were growing up, neither of us had any idea of the heartaches that would soon come our way. We both knew that God had plans for each of them and were anxiously awaiting the moment to see what the plans were. A few years later, when they had grown into men, their ministries finally began.

Chapter 6

The Passover

Once every year, about the middle of spring, we would all go to Jerusalem to observe the Feast of the Passover. My favorite memory of going to the Passover is the year that Jesus had just turned twelve years old. Joseph, Jesus, and I, John and his family, and in fact, almost the entire village and most of the people from the surrounding villages prepared to go to the Passover together that year. It was always a lot of fun and good fellowship as well as a chance to see friends and family that we hadn't seen in a long while. The children could not control themselves; they were filled to the brim with excitement and so eager to help prepare for the journey and the festivities. In fact, they were always, it seemed, on their best behavior.

Passover is an event that has been handed down from generation to generation since our people were held captive in Egypt. Now this is the story behind the yearly Feast of the Passover and why it is so important to us:

Moses was chosen by the Lord God to deliver the people of Israel from out of the Bondage of Egypt. The Pharaoh, or ruler of Egypt, at that time, was very cruel and evil. He hated our people. While being forced to work on his many dangerous projects, many of them had died of starvation, or just from being beaten to death for no reason at all. Public floggings of the slaves was considered entertainment for the Egyptians and any visitors that they may have. Many of the Israelites were just simply too old to handle the long hard work from the early light of morning to dark and then many long hard nights, there was no quitting until it became impossible to see what they were doing.

The Pharaoh did not care because he knew that there were thousands of slaves and the ones who died would be replaced by another and another and each new slave would be made to work even harder to get the job done. The slaves knew that all they could do was to work hard and to stand strong. They knew if they were to become weary and fall, they would surely die.

God sent Moses to Egypt to set His people free. God kept hardening Pharaoh's heart and just as he seemed willing to set the people free, he would change his mind until finally, the tenth time had come. God said that He would send a plague that would end the Israelites being enslaved in Egypt by this cruel, evil man once and for all.

Moses told the people of Israel that the Lord God had said that He would send an "Angel of Death" throughout all the land of Egypt and that all the firstborns in the land would die. From the firstborn of Pharaoh, the cruel ruler, to the firstborn of the maid servant, and even the firstborn of their beasts would die. He said that there would be a great cry throughout all the land as there had never been known nor would ever be known again. But not any one of the firstborn of the children of Israel would be harmed.

God told Moses to tell everyone to take a lamb without blemish, a male of the first year from the sheep or the goats and they were to keep it up and take care of it for two weeks. On that day, the entire congregation of Israel was to kill their lamb in the evening. They were to take its blood and strike it on the two side-posts and the upper door post of their houses, and then they were to eat the lamb. They were to eat it that night with unleavened bread and bitter herbs, and if any of it remained, it was to be burned with fire. The blood on their doors was to show the "Angel of Death" that he was not to touch that house but to "pass over" it that night, when all of Egypt was smitten.

At the late midnight hour, the silence was broken by weeping and wailing that was heard all throughout the land of Egypt. Thousands were mourning their dead. You could hear the women's loud, broken-hearted screams; all the wives, daughters, mothers, and sisters could be heard screaming in agony. Death had left no Egyptian home untouched that night because there was at least one "firstborn" dwelling in every one of them.

The Pharaoh also had a young firstborn son, whom he loved very much. The angel of death had left his mark on the house of Pharaoh as well. In his painful and sorrowful grief, he and his men rose up in the middle of the night and called for Moses and Aaron to come quickly. He had decided to make hast and before the great God of Moses did something else and maybe was caused to become even angrier, he would tell Moses, the deliverer, that now he would let the people go. God had used His servant, Moses, to deliver the people of Israel from the cruel bondage of Egypt that day. That day of freedom has since been a memorial to the Jewish people and we were commanded by the Lord, our God, to keep it a feast to the Lord throughout the generations and an ordinance forever.

Yes, that was indeed one of the greatest nights in history. Thousands of slaves had been set free. A nation was reborn. The Lord God of Israel had delivered again!

Now after the festivities and the Feast of the Passover were completed, it was time for all of us to return to our homes. Joseph and I, along with all our friends and family members, began packing our belongings and getting ready to start our long journeys home. We planned to start on our way at sunrise.

After traveling for a full day, the men found a nice, large spot that was big enough for all of us to make our camps for the night. There was a small lake with a big flat parcel of land surrounding it, and most of the people were more than ready to stop and rest. Some of the children and babies were so tired they had begun to whine, and the women were worn out as well. All of us women found it a great blessing to have such a large camping area with so much water nearby. The children could bathe or swim and everyone would have plenty of water for cooking and cleaning up after dinner.

Joseph and I had made our camp along the side of the lake next to a big rock. When I had finished preparing our evening meal, and we were ready to eat, I went to find Jesus but could not find Him anywhere in the camp. I ran to find John, his closest friend, to see if they were together. John said that he had been trying to find Jesus since we had left Jerusalem early that morning. No one in the entire group had seen Him. I began to panic and could hardly keep from crying. We would simply have to return to Jerusalem to find Him. That was our only choice, and I was hoping that we would meet him on the way trying to catch up to us.

Joseph said it would be better to wait until first light to start our trip back. We were very tired from the day's journey, and if we left without any rest at all, we would not be able to go very far. We decided to try to get just a little nap before starting out again. I couldn't sleep at all. Jesus was only twelve years old, and although very grown up for His age, I could not help worrying about Him. I knew that God would provide shelter, food, and protection for Him, but I still just couldn't bear the thoughts of my "little boy" spending the night by Himself.

Early in the morning, just before daybreak, we hurried to gather up our camp and began our day's journey back to Jerusalem to try to find Jesus. We said goodbye to everyone and started on our way.

As we neared Jerusalem, we asked everyone we met along the way if they had seen a boy about twelve years old anywhere. No one had seen Him. All the way to Jerusalem, we got the same response from everyone whom we would stop to ask, "No, we haven't seen a young boy alone."

Joseph was as worried as I, but he tried to keep it to himself. He knew that if I had any idea of his being worried, I would be terrified. Finally, late in the afternoon, we reached the city once more. We searched and searched for Jesus night and day, and after three days, we were still wearily hoping to find a trace somewhere. Early that morning, as we were walking past the temple, we met an elderly man, and Joseph asked him if he had seen a young boy about twelve years old who seemed to be alone.

He said, "There has been a young man in the temple who has been talking to the doctors and scribes and a lot of the other men who live in the city of Jerusalem. He has such knowledge of the scriptures that He has been amazing everyone who hears Him. No one has ever seen Him here before; although He is very young, He still speaks with great power and authority. I was in the temple listening to Him speak and only left a short time ago. He may still be over there."

That is indeed where we found Jesus, in the temple. He was sitting in the midst of the doctors, both hearing them and asking them questions. Joseph and I were amazed at what we saw. The men with Him were simply dumbfounded. Later, most of them stopped to tell Joseph that he had learned something new from the teachings of Jesus and they all said that they would love to sit with Him again.

I was so happy to see Him and hugging Him, I asked, "Jesus, where were you all this time? How could you do this to us, son? We have been hunting you for four days now and we have been so worried about you. Joseph and I had gone a whole day's journey toward home and had started to eat our evening meal and then we realized that you weren't with John and hadn't even gone with us. We had to make the journey all the way back here to find you and have been in Jerusalem, looking for you for three days. I have been so scared, not knowing if I would ever find you, at least not alive and well. We have looked everywhere and asked everyone whom we met along the way."

Jesus just looked at Joseph and me and then in a soft, sweet, calm voice, He said, "How is it that you sought me? Did you not know that I must be about my Father's business?"

Joseph just shook his head, not completely understanding all that Jesus had said. With a big broad smile on his face, he reached over to Jesus and rubbed the top of His head, then taking His hand, said, "Come now we must go home, we have a lot of work to get done."

All the way home, every day, the two of them played games. They would race, skip around in circles, and zigzag across the dirt road, the entire time giggling and laughing hysterically. They made a long trip fun for all three of us. I enjoyed it as much as they did, just watching them playing together. Sometimes they would make me laugh so hard that I would have tears running down my face. I could see the love that they felt for each other.

We didn't catch up with our friends and neighbors because with their head start, they had already reached their homes. We decided to take our time getting home; we did not have to be in such a big hurry. The work could wait a day or two. We made our camp at the same spot that everyone had chosen days before. Joseph and Jesus went for a cool swim and bath in the small lake, while I prepared our evening meal. After eating their dinner, the two of them decided to do some reading and studying. I cleaned up our mess, and then I left to go down to the pond to wash up. It was almost dark when I had finished washing the dishes and taking a quick bath and returned to our camp. The three of us were becoming tired, and we just wanted to get some rest so that we could start early the next morning.

Three days later, we finally reached home. It was getting late in the evening, and we were so happy to once again sleep in our beds. We were so tired that we went to bed without having our evening meal. We had never slept so late; the sun had already come up. Any other day, Joseph would have left for the carpenter shop hours ago.

Suddenly, Jesus was hugging us awake. He gave us a good morning kiss on our cheek and laughing. He began singing to us, making the song up as He sang, "Now the sun is up, and it's time for you to get up, you better wake up, get up, you two sleepyheads, it is going to be a long, busy morning! There is work to be done, to be done! Now it is up and at it. You will have to wait and sleep tonight!"

We all laughed, hugged each other, and got up to start our day! He always had a way of doing precious little loving things to make our lives so wonderful and kept us laughing all the time. Our home was always filled with God's love and His special blessings.

Soon, Jesus and Joseph were ready to leave for work. They both gave me a big hug and a kiss on the cheek and then they were gone. Still feeling a bit weary from the long journey, I had to make myself get my day started, because knowing that when they came home that evening, they would be hungry and very tired, and there was a lot of cleaning that needed to be done.

I began singing the silly little wake-up song that Jesus had sung to us that morning. I kept smiling and laughing until my eyes would fill with happy tears all throughout the day. I had kept so busy and the day had passed so quickly that before I realized it, I barely had enough time to prepare our evening meal before my men came home from work.

Chapter 7

Cousin John

Sometimes in the early afternoon, just before I would need to start preparing the evening meal for Joseph, I would clean Jesus up a little bit and take Him for a short visit over to see his best friend, John. The boys were about two and a half or three years old maybe, and they loved each other so much that they wanted to play together all the time.

They always played so well and never had a disagreement of any kind. Both Jesus and John loved to draw, and each of them had a little slate and loved to sit together and make pictures of animals. Most of the time, neither Elizabeth nor I had any idea of course, what they had drawn until they told us. Often, they would try teasing us, saying that they were making a sketch of us. They would make the person in the picture have big ears or a long nose like an elephant or spots like a leopard. Giggling, they would ask us if we recognized whom they had drawn. It would turn out to be either Mother Mary or Mother Elizabeth. These two precious little boys kept us laughing all the time. Both boys could be mischievous; however, on occasion, John may have taken a practical joke a bit farther than it should have gone. He was always able to solve any unexpected problem that it may have caused.

Jesus and John had very similar personalities and were very wise for their years. They loved all people and hated cruelty and abuse, and if there was anyone who was hungry or had any sickness, it would just break their hearts. Elizabeth and I knew that we were very blessed as we watched them grow up together, knowing from where they came. We had both realized, from their conceptions, that God had plans for each of them and we were just patiently but maybe a little nervously, waiting to see what those plans were going to be.

Although Jesus and John were like best friends and they were together all throughout their childhood, when the two of them were grown into men, they began to lead separate lives, with each of them having his godly purpose to fulfill. Jesus was still living at home and working in the carpenter shop, and John began living as a hermit in the wilderness.

John began preaching and preparing the way for the Messiah to come into view. He preached, saying, "Repent ye: for the kingdom of heaven is at hand." He was known as the "voice of the one crying in the wilderness." His raiment was of camel hair, and he wore leather girdle about his loins.

John ate locusts and wild honey. Sometimes he took the time to do a little fishing to change his diet. Always upholding the laws of God, he did not care to tell the people about the sins that they were committing, even King Herod, himself. When preaching, John would tell the followers that he baptized them with water, but the one who would come after him would baptize everyone with the Holy Ghost and with fire. He also preached that he was not worthy to unlatch this "One's" sandals. He told them to repent, and then he would baptize them into repentance.

One morning, Jesus came from Galilee to the River of Jordan to be baptized by John. When John looked out and saw Him walking toward him into the water, he said, "Behold the Lamb of God, which taketh away the sins of the world!"

Jesus always loved lambs because they were so lowly and submissive and never could be provoked. I always thought it was so fitting that when He became a man, He was called "the Lamb of God"! Yet while He was hanging on the cross, the detailed comparison was exact.

After John had baptized Him and brought Him up out of the water, the heavens opened, and the Spirit of God descended upon Him like a dove, and a voice from heaven was heard saying, "This is my beloved Son, in whom I am well pleased." Immediately following His being baptized by John, Jesus left and went into the wilderness alone to fast for forty days. He was being prepared by the Father to do the work that He had come to the earth to do. The Baptism of Jesus was the last time that He and John would be together while on earth. However, after their deaths, they would be reunited in the Kingdom of Heaven.

A few weeks later, while John was preaching and baptizing in the River of Jordan, King Herod, his wife, Herodias, and his teenaged stepdaughter, who was also his niece, Salome, came along the path by the river. They had stopped for a short time to both hear him preach and were also hoping to find some reason to mock him.

Many who were in the multitude of followers said on seeing them arrive that John had run across the shallow water of the Jordan River and up to the side of the king's chariot. He was boldly screaming to Herod and Herodias that they must repent. He was accusing them of having committed the sin of adultery. He said that it was no secret that Herod had taken his brother Phillip's wife, Herodias, long before his brother had died. John had loudly proclaimed these accusations, as his multitude of followers stood listening nearby on the banks of the Jordan River.

Both Herod and Herodias were extremely angry with him because he had dared speak these evil words against the king's family and especially in front of the large multitude of witnesses who were standing there. The young daughter, Salome, had never heard such cruel things spoken about her mother. Of course, they had later convinced her that all of what John had said was a pack of vicious lies to discredit the king and his family. After all, who would want to believe that her mother could do anything so sinful?

From that moment on, the two of them secretly planned in their evil minds to get "rid" of John. Some man in the crowd had said that he had heard Herod's wife pleading with him to stop the chariot right at that very moment and to "cut" out John's tongue so that he could not spread any more hateful lies about her. However, everyone except for their young daughter knew for a fact that everything John had said was true. The same man also heard Herod tell her that if he even tried to harm John in front of this great multitude of his followers, that the chariot in which they were riding would probably be turned upside down and burned to the ground leaving the three of them tied in it to be burned alive. He cracked the whip and made the horses gallop as fast as they could go. He wanted to leave the baptist, his followers, and the accusations behind. A lot of the men thought that he had suddenly became frightened and, since they were alone, wanted to get his family to safety.

About a week or so later, we had heard from one of John's disciples that the king had sent soldiers out to arrest John right in front of his followers and his disciples and led him off to be put into prison. From that time on, I began to fear for his life. I knew that Herodias was even more cruel-hearted than her husband, King Herod, and that her hatred would only end with John's being killed. I was afraid that she would pay someone to murder him behind the king's back, perhaps one of the guards or even one of the prisoners.

I knew from the beginning when Elizabeth and I were visiting, after both of us had become pregnant, that God also had plans for her son, John, as well as my "son" Jesus.

Of course, I had always known that Jesus was the "Son of God" and that I would have to share Him because he was not only mine, but He belonged to the whole world forever.

Soon after John's death, Jesus began preaching and baptizing, doing what His Heavenly Father had sent Him to earth to do. That is when I realized the part that John had been sent to play, indeed, he was to be the forerunner of the Gospel for Him.

After His stay in the wilderness, Jesus stopped by my home to say goodbye because when He had heard that John had been put into prison, He decided to go to Galilee for a little while, thinking that His life too was in danger. Soon after He arrived, and we were having our evening meal, one of John's disciples stopped in to tell us the horrible news that John was no longer in prison, but dead. He had been beheaded the night before. The man was so upset that tears were building up in his eyes as he was speaking to us. We were all devastated. Although being very hurt and maybe somewhat angry with the evil ones who were responsible for the brutal death of His dear friend John, Jesus gave comfort to us all, saying that he was now with God and his work had been well done, and God was well pleased with him.

Later in the day, we heard what had the reason been for the horrific death of our beloved John. Just as I had been praying for him and worrying that something bad would happen to him in prison, it had. Herod's evil minded wife, Herodias, was devising a demonic plan of her own to take his life. She had vowed to get even with him from the day of his preaching to her at the Jordan River and spreading what she had called "the vicious lies" and now the wicked queen had schemed and lied her way into concocting a plan to be finally able to do just that. Herod had only ordered John's arrest, hoping to satisfy Herodias. He was hoping that in a few weeks, she would be over her mad spell, and he could quietly have him set free. He also thought that his having been arrested would scare him so badly that he would not ever even think of mentioning the name of Herod or any of his family again when he was preaching to his followers.

Of course, Herodias had other ideas. It was the king's birthday and seeing a chance to both make him happy because of his love for attention and at the same time to get even with John, Herodias ordered the servants to prepare a great birthday celebration for him. All the important people throughout the land were to be invited. She had made a large guest list and planned an even larger feast.

Salome, the daughter of Herodias, was very beautiful and almost as evil as her mother, the queen. She and her mother wanted to add a very special birthday surprise for their king. Salome would wait until he was in his normal drunken stupor and then she would dance and slowly undress for him and his guests.

Of course, because of his being in a drunken state, Herod's lust became uncontrollable. He was so blinded by the beauty of the young woman that he promised her, on oath, and in front of all, of his guests, to give her anything whatsoever she would ask, even as much as half of his kingdom.

Now earlier, when the two wicked women were making plans for the birthday celebration, Salome and Herodias decided to take their evil surprise a bit farther. Knowing Herod's weaknesses very well, and knowing that during his celebrating he would become so drunk that he could be easily persuaded by the beautiful young girl. Herodias told Salome exactly what she should ask as payment for her dance. Since the Baptist had told such hateful, shameful lies about her mother (which were all true) and had made her look like a cheap harlot, she should ask Herod for the crazy prophet's head in a charger.

Later, at the celebration, when she had finished her dance and was promised "her heart's desire," she then made her request known to the king.

She leaned over and kissed him on the lips and then with an enticing smile, bowed to him. Kneeling at his feet and still smiling seductively, she said, "Oh your royal majesty and my beloved king. I could only ask that for your beautiful daughter's gift of anything that her heart would desire, that you would please have brought to me this night, the head of the vicious liar who is known as John the Baptist in a charger."

Beginning to sober up a bit, Herod realized the promise that he had made to her. He was very sorry for asking her wishes, but nevertheless, for the oath's sake and for all of them who were seated there with him, he had no choice but to order the terrible deed to be done.

He sent a small group of his most loyal soldiers to the prison, and there, that very night, he had them to behead John. An hour or so later, one of the soldiers walked into the palace, down the corridor, into the ballroom, and right in front of the party guests, he handed the charger with John's head to Salome. With a broad smile, she took it and turned away from the crowd, and she presented the charger to her mother, Herodias, the evil queen.

The entire room rang with laughter. Most of the men were quite intoxicated and, seeing the head, caused them to go into a frenzy. They became very loud and were joking, screeching, singing, dancing around the room, and pointing to the head. The foolish, evildoers believed that they had silenced the mouth of the innocent prophet, and his "vicious rumors" forever.

Then although everyone was growing tired from partying, one of the men stood up in front of the crowd and said that they should celebrate the death of the "troublemaker" and have another drink for that. Laughing and dancing and being merry, they were acting as if they had just begun.

Herodias and Salome, after doing their evil deed, were tired so they just went to bed and fell asleep. The two women felt no remorse and had no bad feelings at all about what they just had done.

An hour or so later, in the evening, just before sundown, some of John's disciples went to the prison and were given permission to take John's body and bury it. I do not recall hearing anything about their having gone to King Herod's palace and taking John's head to be buried also.

That was only the beginning of the many tragedies and sorrows that were to follow and to break my heart. Again, I spent a lot of time trying to console poor Elizabeth; she was devastated to the point that she was almost unable to speak. Like all of us, she just could not believe that something so cruel had happened to her son, John. He had never done anything to hurt anyone. All he did was preach God's word and beg the people to repent of their sins.

Chapter 8

Jesus Picked Twelve

Jesus had many disciples throughout His adult life. There were some who followed Him in secret because they were afraid of making the Jews angry. There was a group of about seventy men who also claimed to be His disciples. He had many close followers who loved Him with all their hearts and would walk with Him obeying all His teachings and loving Him all along the way. He had chosen a special group of twelve godly men of whom He knew would be by His side at any time and would leave everything they had, including friends and family and just simply "follow Him"!

Eleven of the disciples, of which all the twelve were men, were from the area around Galilee but Judas Iscariot (who later betrayed Jesus, selling Him for thirty pieces of silver) who was also the treasurer for the group, was from Judea. These men were all fishermen except for Matthew, who was a tax collector. Still, as he was chosen, each of them gave up his way of living, home, family, job, and as Jesus said, "Denied himself and took up his cross and followed Him."

All the twelve men, except Judas, were very loyal to Jesus, loved Him very much and were always ready to help the needy in any way they could. Jesus had said that the needy were the poor, the sick, the blind, the deaf and dumb, the lepers, the sinners, all the poor people who were demon possessed, and the ones who just felt alone and hopelessly useless.

The first two disciples chosen were Andrew and his brother, Simon Peter. Andrew had been a disciple of John who was called "The Baptist" because of his baptizing the people to repent of their sins. John had called Jesus as he was baptizing Him "The Lamb of God." Now Andrew had heard Jesus speaking and was very enthusiastic about Him. He went and found his brother, Simon Peter, and brought him to see Jesus.

When Peter saw Jesus, he said, "Behold the Christ, the Son of the Living God!" Jesus then called Peter "The Rock." That day Jesus told Andrew and Peter to leave everything and follow Him. Having been filled with the Holy Spirit, they were happy to become His disciples. Both men were fishermen by trade and Jesus told them that now, they would be "fishers of men."

The third disciple was Phillip. Jesus went into Galilee and saw him and told him to follow Him and immediately Phillip stood up and went with Jesus. Phillip also found his friend, Nathanael, and told him that he was following Jesus of Nazareth, of whom the prophets wrote in the Scriptures. When Nathanael saw Him, he said, "Rabbi, thou art the Son of God; thou art the King of Israel."

Now Jesus had chosen four men, who knew Him to be the Christ, the Messiah. Andrew and his brother Peter, who Jesus called the rock, and Phillip and Nathanael, who was also known as Bartholomew, were very willing to follow Him. After calling these four men, Jesus continued to select another eight men to become the twelve chosen disciples. They followed Him to His death, and then afterward, they continued to preach His word until their deaths. All four were very honest, faithful, and eager to learn.

Peter, however, was a little arrogant and sometimes hardheaded; at times, he was even hot-tempered, but he was also tenderhearted. A few times, he had to be reprimanded, but Jesus knew that he loved Him unconditionally and Jesus loved him as much.

As a matter of fact, all of us loved Peter. He was the only disciple of the twelve who was married. His wife was a very special woman and understood his destiny. She would patiently wait at home for weeks for Peter to return for a day or so, or she would be found in the crowd of followers who were walking with Jesus, or at the women's quarters lending a helping hand. She knew from experience who Jesus was because her mother and Peter's mother-in-law was one of the many healing miracles that Jesus would later perform. She had a very high fever and Jesus just touched her hand, and the fever left her, and at that moment, she got out of bed and began to help Peter's wife minister unto Jesus and the disciples.

Then there were the two Zebedee brothers, James and probably Jesus's favorite of all, John. He called them the sons of thunder. They were both fishermen and had a business with their father, but they left him to handle it alone as they went to follow Jesus. These young men were both rather selfish but courageous and loving as well. They loved to tease and were always laughing. They were with Jesus in the Garden of Gethsemane and sat with Him at the Last Supper. Yes, James and John were faithful to Jesus and preached His word for the rest of their lives.

Another disciple was Matthew. He was a tax collector in Galilee. Jesus just past by Matthew's little shed where he was collecting taxes and all He said was "Follow me." Matthew stood up and left everything behind and followed Him from then to His death.

Then there was Thomas. Yes, precious Thomas, a man who had to see as he said, "with my own eyes" before he would believe almost anything. He doubted everything, even a lot of times after having been able to "see" for himself. Bless his heart, he just couldn't and wouldn't put his trust in anything or anyone except he did believe that Jesus was the Son of God. Months later, after the disciples and Jesus had become very comfortable walking and witnessing together, the other eleven began to jokingly call him "Doubting Thomas." That nickname stayed with him until after Jesus had risen from the dead. After what he had seen that day, most of his doubting was over.

Yes, although he was doubtful, he was faithful to Jesus to the end. He truly loved Jesus, and he knew that He was the Christ. That was one thing that He had neither questioned nor had ever "doubted."

After the crucifixion and Jesus had risen from the dead, Doubting Thomas, as he was called, at least throughout Jesus's ministry, had to touch the wounds in Jesus's hands and His side before he was able to believe that it was He, Jesus, who had risen and was indeed standing there before him alive. Then suddenly he proclaimed, "My Lord and My God!"

Last but equally just as important were James, Thaddaeus, and Simon, three men who truly loved Jesus and were faithful to Him with all their hearts.

Then there was Judas Iscariot, the one who proved to be untrue, the traitor! He followed Jesus all the way to His death. In fact, he played a big part in having Him arrested, condemned, and sentenced to death on the cross; yet still, the entire time, proclaiming his loyalty to Him. The same unfaithful, deceitful man, who had been or at least, everyone had thought that he was a trusted friend. He was one of the twelve chosen disciples and had walked with Jesus every day, yet a few years later, he sold Him for thirty pieces of silver and betrayed Him with a kiss on His cheek, which ultimately lead to His crucifixion only a couple of days after His arrest.

Judas was also the treasurer for the group, although he was very unscrupulous, selfish, dishonest, and evil, the other eleven disciples did not notice and even though he was somewhat hateful and haughty in nature, they could overlook his short comings, and they all became very close friends. Unfortunately, to our dismay, after he betrayed Jesus, we learned that he was also the devil in the flesh. We had not given much thought to His personality until after everything was all over, and we were thinking and talking about Judas. We then remembered that there were a few things that seemed always to make him very angry.

For instance, little children got on his nerves, and when they were near, he would usually leave for a couple of hours. He wouldn't say anything but just disappear. They would make him angry if the only racket that they were making was their laughter. He just could not stand being around them. He said that they caused a big disturbance wherever they were. He had a very cruel streak about him because he had also been known to have kicked some of the pack animals a time or two, especially if they were to stumble or he thought that they weren't walking fast enough. Jesus didn't see him, and no one ever told Him what he had done. He also hated the elderly and thought that they were in the way of the younger people and caused too much trouble.

We all began to realize that he seemed to have hated everything and everybody for some reason or another. Now, thinking back, I don't remember a time when I was near him that he was not murmuring or complaining about something, and I don't ever remember seeing him smile the entire time that he followed Jesus. I did hear, however, that he had a broad smile on his face while he was betraying Him with the "kiss." Later, everyone began to call the betrayal of a friend the "Judas kiss."

No one could remember ever seeing him doing anything that was unkind to anyone during the time that he followed Jesus in the ministry. Someone said later that he was as sly as an old fox. We do remember, however, that he never wanted to give anything to the poor or to help them in anyway. He said that they were poor because they chose to be because they refused to work.

Judas was chosen to be a part of Jesus's life because he, too, fit into God's plan of salvation for mankind. I also believe that there is a lesson to be learned from his betrayal, and that is, "Everyone is not always the person whom he professes to be."

I was very blessed to be among these amazing, and powerful men of God that is the other eleven chosen disciples, both ministering to them with food and sometimes even helping with washing their clothes. They were all so very special to me, and I knew that they were completely devoted to "my" son. They always treated me, as well as everyone whom they would meet, with love and respect. I was called "Mother Mary" by all of them, and I felt as if I had gained eleven more sons.

One day, Jesus sent the disciples forth and told them to go to the lost sheep of Israel and preach to them. He gave them the power to heal the sick, open the eyes of the blind, and to touch the mouths of the dumb and make them talk. He also gave them the ability to touch the lame and make them walk and to touch the deaf and make them hear. Jesus said that they could cleanse the lepers, cast out devils, and even on a couple of occasions, raise people from the dead. He taught them how to preach and how to be a servant of the Lord. He also told to teach all nations, baptizing them in the name of the Father, and of the Son, and of the Holy Ghost. He told them to be careful and to always let the Spirit of the Father speak through them. He told them that they would be hated of all men because He was hated.

They all knew that they had chosen a perilous journey, but also, they knew that the road that they were traveling would end in everlasting peace and harmony. The disciples of Jesus found complete joy and felt very blessed in knowing that they would, later, spend an eternity in Heaven with Jesus, the Christ, the only Begotten Son of the Living God and His Father! Their goal was, simply, to please Jesus and to always be found doing His will. Each one of the eleven disciples reached His goal and proved to be faithful to the end.

Chapter 9

The Ministry Begins

Soon after being baptized by John, Jesus went into the wilderness to fast. He had some things that He had to sort out in His mind so that he could begin living the life that Father-God had sent Him to earth to live. He stayed alone in the wilderness for forty days and forty nights and did not eat or drink. In His weakened state, His hunger presented Satan with the opportunity to tempt Him while He was praying. Jesus quoted the Scriptures to him and said, "Get thee behind me, Satan, for it is written, Thou shalt not tempt the Lord thy God." Seeing that he could not persuade Jesus with his foolish enticements, Satan ended the temptations and left.

The next morning, Jesus returned in the power of the Spirit of God. Learning of the cruel fate that John had met, He departed for Galilee. There He began preaching and teaching multitudes of people in the land just beyond the River of Jordan that was called the Galilee of the Gentiles. Jesus was about thirty years old when he began His ministry.

A few months later, Jesus stopped at home and invited me to go to listen to His preaching. I was so excited and felt so blessed to be with my grown "son" once again. From that day on, I was usually among the multitudes of people who followed Him from city to city.

He began preaching as did John, saying, "Repent: for the kingdom of heaven is at hand."

He taught them saying:

"Blessed are the poor in spirit, for theirs is the kingdom of heaven. Blessed are they that mourn; for they shall be comforted. Blessed are the meek: for they shall inherit the earth. Blessed are they which do hunger and thirst after righteous: for they shall be filled. Blessed are the merciful: for they shall obtain mercy. Blessed are the pure in heart: for they shall see God. Blessed are the peacemakers: for they shall be called the children of God. Blessed are they which are persecuted for righteousness sake: for theirs is the kingdom of heaven" (Matt. 5:3-10).

Then He sat down and still teaching told the multitude to rejoice and be exceedingly glad: for great would be their reward in heaven. He always preached love and honor for everyone.

While sitting with the multitude, He reminded them of the Ten Commandments and how important it was to live by them. He said that these had been handed down since Moses had delivered the children of Israel out of the bondage of Egypt. He preached that keeping the commandments was the way of righteousness, and it was the only way to prepare for life eternal with the Father in heaven. He said that the first commandment was the greatest one of them all: "Thou shalt love the Lord thy God with all thy heart, and with all thy soul, and with all thy mind." And then he said the second one was like unto it: "Thou shalt love thy neighbor as thyself." Everywhere that He went to preach and to teach, He always told the people that the most important part of your life is to love your fellowman and to treat him the way that you want to be treated.

He then told them that the other commandments were very valuable to follow as well: "Thou shalt not steal. Thou shalt do no murder. Thou shalt not commit adultery. Thou shalt not bear false witness against thy neighbor. Thou shalt not covet anything that is thy neighbors. Thou shalt have no other gods before Me. Honor thy father and thy mother. Thou shalt not take the name of the Lord, thy God in vain."

During His ministry, His teachings amazed the multitudes and His fame spread throughout the land. Hundreds of people were added daily to His large group of followers.

Every day someone would have a new question for Him. One man asked Him if a person keeps doing you a wrong over and over, how many times should you be able to forgive him?

Jesus simply smiled and said, "you must forgive him seventy times seven" (490 times). Another time, He told one of the men that; it is better to give than to receive. The man had a puzzled look on his face at first, but then suddenly, after pondering on His words for a minute, he smiled and said, "Oh yes, now I understand," and he just backed up and sat down on the ground continuing to listen to the rest of the sermon.

In one of His sermons, Jesus was talking about praying. He told them that the Father knows what you need before you ask of Him and then He told them how they were to pray: He said these exact words:

> Our Father which art in heaven, Hallowed be thy name. Thy kingdom come. Thy will be done in earth, as it is in heaven. Give us this day our daily bread. And forgive us our debts, as we forgive our debtors. And lead us not into temptation, but deliver us from evil: For thine is the kingdom, and the power, and the glory, forever. Amen (Matt. 6:9-13).

Right after he had told them how to pray, He said, "For if ye forgive men their trespasses, your heavenly Father will also forgive you: But if ye forgive not men their trespasses, neither will your Father forgive your trespasses."

I saw the many miracles that He performed. Since the moment of conception, I, knowing who He was, would still be amazed at the miraculous works that He did, and I learned something new every day from His teachings. He had many friends but He also had as many enemies. Satan worked as hard spreading evil and sowing discontentment; as Jesus worked doing good and sowing love for one another.

I remember one incident of treachery and hypocrisy very well. It concerned a poor woman who was brought to Jesus by a group of the scribes and Pharisees. They said that she had been taken in the very act of adultery.

Everyone was sitting around talking and fellowshipping. Jesus was taking a short break when suddenly, an eerie hush came over the crowd. We looked out toward the roadway and saw a young woman who was being dragged through the gravels and bushes by a small group of men. When the group reached Jesus, the two men who were dragging her just threw her to the ground at the feet of Jesus for Him to pass judgment on her. I felt so sorry for her, I could hardly keep from crying. The poor thing was dirty and her black hair was matted and sticking to the sides of her face. Her face had been scratched by the bushes and she was bleeding from her nose and mouth. Her eyes were swollen almost shut. The purple robe that she wore was mud-caked, badly wrinkled, and torn. She had a look of terror on her face. Every man who was a part of the group carried a large stone in his hand. I am sure that she expected that at any minute, the stones would begin hurling toward her face and she would be instantly killed.

The one big robust man who was dragging her from her right side seemed to be the leader of the group, he said, in a rather mocking voice, "Master, this woman was taken in the very act of adultery. Now Moses in the law commanded us that such should be stoned, but what do you say that we should do with her?" By saying these words, the man was hoping that someday, the answer Jesus had given to him could be used against Him.

Instead of answering them, Jesus stooped down and with His finger began to write in the dirt on the ground, as though He hadn't heard them. They continued to ask Him, "Will you not tell us what we should do with her? Please give us an answer!"

He then stood up and pausing for a couple of minutes, looked in the eyes of each one of them. He said, "He that is without sin among you, let him first cast a stone at her."

Again, He stooped down and began to write with His finger on the ground. We could not see what He had written and none of us ever asked Him. The men may have seen, and that could have been the reason they had left so abruptly.

After hearing what Jesus had to say, and being convicted by their own consciences, each man dropped his stone and turned and went out one by one, from the eldest to the last. They never, not one of them, looked back toward Jesus and the poor woman. Jesus and the woman had been left by themselves, surrounded by the midst of His followers.

The poor woman was sobbing loudly. Her tears had wet her face and were falling on the ground. Standing up, Jesus looked in the woman's eyes, and with a compassionate smile, He said, "Woman where are those, thine accusers?"

And the woman looking around about them answered him saying, "There is no one, Lord!"

And Jesus said to her, "Neither do I condemn thee, go and sin no more."

The woman could not believe what she had heard. She had never seen such compassion. She had been saved from death by stoning. She then sat down near Him and listened to Him preach and teach the crowd of followers, and from that day on, she was usually among the multitudes who followed Him and was always willing to help in any way she could.

Everywhere He would go, there were those who tried to trick Him and accuse Him of being a devil and of blasphemer. Many of them were doing everything they could to discredit Him, but God was always there to protect His Son. Some of them were making accusations about Him because He was always sitting, talking, and sometimes, eating with the sinners. He would always just smile compassionately and would always answer their questions with a question: He asked them, "Does a healthy man have need of a physician, I think not, but only a sick man; and the same is with a Righteous man, he has already believed, but it is the sinner who needs a Savior!" Having heard these things, the men turned and although very angry, silently left.

One Sabbath, Jesus had walked through a corn field. He and His disciples stopped and plucked a few ears of corn for Him and His hungry disciples to eat. Some of the Pharisees saw Him and accused Him of breaking the law. Also, some of them had seen the disciples and Jesus eating some of their meals without having washed their hands. It was the tradition of the elders for all the men of the Pharisees, the Scribes, and all the Jews to wash their hands before eating. They began to criticize Him again.

Jesus told them that what goes into a man does not defile him but what comes out of the man. He said that from within, out of the heart of men, proceeds evil thoughts, adulteries, murders, fornications, thefts, deceit, covetousness, wickedness, an evil eye, blasphemies, lasciviousness, pride, and foolishness. The Pharisees were angered by His words and went their way seeking a plan to destroy Him. Peter, one of Jesus disciples, shared one of his favorite memories with me and he told me about one afternoon when he, the other disciples, and Jesus were on a boat out in the middle of the sea. The sky became darkened and suddenly, a terrible storm came up. The harsh wind was blowing so hard that the boat was being tossed back and forth. Once or twice they thought it looked as if it was going to capsize and drown them all. The disciples were all becoming terrified because the boat was beginning to fill with water.

Jesus was in the back, asleep on a pillow. Being terrified, they awakened Him and told Him that they were all about to be drowned. He stood up, held out His hand, and said, "Peace, be still!" Immediately, the wind ceased, and there was a great calm over the sea. And then He said to them, "Where is your faith, how could you be so afraid?" They were amazed and said, "Even the wind and the sea obey this Man." Another afternoon, when the disciples had gone out in their boat to fish and were in the middle of the sea; they saw what they thought was a spirit walking on water coming toward them. Again, they were afraid but Jesus spoke to them and said, "Fear not, it is I, Jesus." Then Peter asked Him to let him walk on the water too. Jesus reached His hand toward him, and Peter stepped out of the boat and began to walk. Astonished to find himself, being able to walk on the water, he looked down at his feet, and suddenly he began to sink. He called out to Jesus to please save him. Jesus reached out and took his hand, and He and Peter stepped back into the boat and sat down. They, along with the other disciples, sailed over to the shore, and while Peter and John tied up the boat, some of the others took the small bucket of fish that a couple of them had caught before the storm came up, built a fire, and began to cook their evening meal.

Jesus kept preaching to the multitudes and He said to those Jews who believed in Him. "If you continue in my word, then you are my disciples indeed; and you shall know the truth, and the truth shall set you free. Verily, Verily, I say unto you, whosoever commits sin is the servant of sin and the servant abide not in the house forever; but the Son abides ever. If the Son therefore shall make you free, you shall be free indeed."

People were always asking Jesus questions about the kingdom of Heaven. One of the disciples asked Him, "Who is the greatest in the kingdom of heaven?" Jesus called a little child up to Him and took him in His arms and hugging him said, "Except you be converted, and become as little children, you shall not enter into the kingdom of heaven. Therefore, whosoever shall humble himself as this little child, the same is greatest in heaven." He would always immediately try to give easily understood answers to all their questions.

One Sabbath day, Jesus entered in their synagogue, and He was asked a question concerning the Sabbath. Just inside, He had met a man with a withered hand. The Pharisees hoping for a chance to trick Him into doing or saying something that they could use against Him, asked Him this question: "Is it not unlawful to heal on the Sabbath?"

He turned to them and said," Is it lawful to do good on the Sabbath days, or to do evil, to save a life, or to kill? What man shall there be among you, that shall have one sheep and if it falls into a pit on the Sabbath day, will he not lay hold on it, and lift it out? How much then is a man better than a sheep? Wherefore it is lawful to do well on the Sabbath Days" (Mark 3:4).

Then he said to the man, "Stretch forth thine hand." He stretched it forth and it was immediately made whole just like his other hand. When the Pharisees had seen this, they angrily left out of the synagogue and held council against Him, seeking to destroy Him once and for all!

I am sure that His easily understood sermons, and the love that everyone could they feel from Him were the reasons why He had so many loyal followers.

I have said over and over, that Jesus had never become angry with anyone, but I do remember that one of His disciples told me otherwise. He had been in His ministry for several months and had many followers, and it was time again for the Jewish Passover. He went to Jerusalem, as He always did to celebrate the event and He had gone to the Temple. Just as He walked in the door, He found that the Jews were selling oxen, sheep, and doves, and a good deal of money was changing hands. He did become very angry at these people indeed, and He took some small cords that He saw laying nearby on a table, and He made a scourge out of them. Then He began to whip the money changers out of the temple. He opened the cages and let the doves fly away and ran some of the animals out. Then, He said to them, "Take these things hence; make not my Father's house a house of merchandise." He also told some of them that the temple was a place of worship and they had made it a den of thieves, and that the marketplace was for selling these things not the Temple of God. He turned over the tables and poured out the money changers money and told them to get their things and go.

Of course, this gave the Jews and Pharisees more reason; to want to rid themselves of Him once and for all. They were very angry with Him and said, "Who does He think He is! He really must think that God has given Him the right to do this. He has made us to look like fools long enough."

Many evenings after preaching and teaching all day, Jesus and His disciples would go over to the Sea of Galilee. They would get in a boat and go out into the middle of the deep to fish. When they came back to land, they would build a fire to prepare a quick meal for themselves. Mary and I always tried to make sure that we had baked them enough bread for them to eat each day. Afterward, they would sit and talk for a while, and then after having their evening prayers, would each spread their cloak or a small blanket on the rough ground and fall asleep. They very seldom slept at home or even in a bed. The next morning; they would arise just before the break of day and get ready for another long day.

Chapter 10

Performing Miracles

Jesus performed so many miracles during His walk on earth that I doubt there would be enough paper available to write all of them down. I went along with Him very often as He was preaching and teaching and I saw many of the miracles that He performed. I was always there with Him when His ministry would keep Him close, but I did not journey out too far from my home.

Each day the crowd would be larger. The followers would come earlier, and earlier each day wanting to catch a glimpse of Jesus and see him perform or even be a part of one of His miracles. Many were just sick and afflicted, and many were demon possessed. There were also many who did not believe in Him, but who would follow at length; hoping to catch just one small thing that they could use against Him. They were wanting to prove Him to be a fake; of the devil, or a blasphemer, and to see Him dead. Many times, I had feared for my "son's life."

Many times, there were people who would point at me and say, "Ask her, what makes Him think that He is the Son of God? Did she not carry Him in her womb for nine months? Does that not mean that He is human? He has a human mother, and Joseph the carpenter is His Father." Then they would sneer, laugh, and just walk away, shaking their heads and murmuring.

It was times like those that my mind would go back to the evening that the angel of the Lord first visited me and I would just smile and say, "Thank you, God, for this Blessing!" Although my heart would break at the accusations and the mockery, I knew that "the people did not know what they were doing." It was so hard for the human mind to comprehend.

I was blessed to be present when he performed His first miracle. It was at a wedding being held in Cana of Galilee. The bridegroom was our cousin and both Jesus and I were invited.

I had been making two little wine cups for a few days and planned to give them as a bridal gift to the bride and groom at the wedding. I had put them on a table in the dining room area.

Jesus stopped in to visit with me for a while, and as he passed the table, He picked up the little cup that I had made for the bride and smiling at me said, "What are these cups? They are so pretty and delicate."

I said, "Those are a gift for your cousin. We are going to a wedding tonight. We have both been invited. There is to be a nice dinner afterward, and the weather is so warm that they are going to have everything in the garden behind their house. You must go too, or they will be so disappointed."

"Oh, that sounds like we will have a lot of fun," Jesus answered. Then pointing toward the door, He said, "What about my friends, Matthew and John, do you think it would be all right to bring them along with us. That is only two more!" Then laughing, He said, "They will behave!"

"Of course," I said, "that would be fine, they are welcome to come along." We all walked over to the garden to join the large crowd that was already gathering for the wedding and everyone had planned to stay afterward for the marriage feast as the reception was called.

Everything was so glorious, decorated so lovely and bright. The bride herself was the most beautiful of all. As soon as the ceremony was over, the feast began. The delicious food was plentiful, and the huge decorated cake was gorgeous. Everyone was talking and laughing and dancing to the music, and suddenly, one of the men said, "We are out of wine, and there is nowhere we can get any at this hour. We have more guests than we had expected. What are we going to do?"

Naturally, I turned to Jesus. I said, "Jesus, there is no wine."

He said, "Woman, what have I to do with thee? Mine hour has not yet come."

He turned back to the men and continued his conversation with them. I told the servants that they must do whatever He told them to do. They asked Him again. There were six water jars of stone sitting on the big table, and He told the servants to fill all six with water. The vessels would hold about nine gallons each. They filled all of them to the brim. He told them to draw out some of it and take it to the governor of the feast.

When the ruler of the feast had tasted the water that had been made into wine, he had no idea of the miracle that had just happened. He called the bridegroom over to his table and asked him why they were getting the good wine last. It was always the custom to serve the best wine first.

Turning the water to wine was the first of many of the fabulous miracles that Jesus performed during His ministry of the last three and a third years of His life walking the earth as a man.

Peter and John had told me that early one morning, Jesus and His disciples had gone out in the middle of the sea on one of the large fishing boats to get away from everyone for a little while. They wanted to get some rest and maybe to do a bit of fishing. Jesus had decided to go to the back of the boat to take a short nap. Suddenly the sky began to darken, the wind began blowing furiously, and the storm was getting so bad that it was causing the calm water to become a raging sea.

The waves had started roaring and getting higher and higher. The huge boat was being tossed from side to side.

Once it almost turned over and then water began pouring into the large craft. It had completely covered the floor and was getting deeper and deeper. The disciples had not brought any pots or vessels of any size along with them that could be used for bailing out the water. They had sailed too far out into the sea to even hope to be able to safely swim back to land if the huge boat were to sink or to capsize. It looked as if the entire crew would surely be drowned. Completely terrified, the disciples decided that their only hope was to awaken Jesus and ask Him for help because; He always had known what to do every time they ran into trouble.

Peter ran over to Him yelling as he went, "Master, Master, you must wake up or else we shall all perish in this raging storm! You have to do something!"

Jesus calmly sat up and looking at Peter, He turned to the sea and rebuked the wind and said unto the sea, "Peace, be still!" and immediately the wind ceased, and there was a great calm. Then sitting back down on the floor of the huge boat, He turned to His disciples and said to them, "Why were you so afraid? Where is your faith?"

They were again afraid and then said to one another, "What manner of man is this, that even the wind and the sea obey His words?" Jesus amazed them so often with all of the miracles that they watched Him perform.

One of the disciples had told me that he, Peter, James, and John and some other men were out fishing. They had tried and tried casting out their nets hoping to get them loaded with fish and had been fishing all night and had caught nothing. Finally, early in the morning, they had given up. Jesus walked up to them and said, "Go out once again and cast into the very deepest part of the sea."

Peter said that they had toiled all night and received nothing, but they would try again by His word. The fishermen went back out into the shallow part of the sea and cast their nets once more. When they cast again and did according to what Jesus had told them, the nets became so full of fish that they began to break. The men called to the other men in the boat that had gone out with them and asked for their help. Both boats were filled and were about to sink. When they had brought their boats safely to land, having never caught so many fish before, they all decided to leave everything and follow Jesus. Everyone was so amazed at the power of God that this man had. He told them that He would make them fishers of men.

Most of the people in the multitudes who followed Jesus believed in Him. They heard His preaching and teaching and saw all the work that He did. Naturally, there were a few skeptics, but they would either soon believe or just leave altogether.

Another time, a poor woman, bless her heart, had been suffering from a bleeding disorder for more than twelve long years. She was pale, weak, and haggard from losing so much blood.

When I noticed her, she was crawling up behind Jesus. She reached out her thin, bony hand and touched the very hem of His robe, and suddenly she stood straight up, and the color immediately came into her precious face, and she was no longer pale and haggard. She looked like a different person standing there.

Jesus then turned and asked, "Who touched me?" for He had felt strength and healing leave His body. The poor woman became terrified. She stepped closer to Him, and she said, "It was I, Lord. I knew that if I could only touch the hem of your garment, that I would forever be made whole!" He looked at her and then He said, "Daughter, be of good comfort; thy faith had made the whole!" She had been healed immediately.

One afternoon, Jesus walked into a ruler's house, and the people inside were playing music and making the death march, and Jesus told them that the maid was not dead, only sleeping and the people laughed and sneered at Him as they often did. He took her by the hand and she arose, both alive and well.

As he left the home, two blind men had begun to follow Him, crying out to Him and begging Him to touch their eyes, as He had done for so many others, that they would be able to see. He immediately turned toward them and reaching out to them, touched their eyes, and told them that it was their faith that had opened their eyes and given them their sight.

Jesus had been preaching all day, and it was getting late in the afternoon so we started preparing to leave Jericho. It was Jesus, His disciples, me, Mary, and the usual loyal multitude who had always followed Him everywhere that He would go. There was also that day, a great number of new people who had decided to come along with us. Walking down the highway, we encountered a poor blind man sitting by the side of the road begging. He was holding a dirty, broken cup out to us, hoping that someone would put in a coin or two. Some of the people in our group recognized him as the man who sat there every day from daylight until almost dark. The man was called Blind Bartimaeus by everyone who knew him because he had been blinded from birth.

As the crowd was walking by, the poor blind man had heard someone mention the name of Jesus. Having heard rumors that He was the famed healer, Jesus of Nazareth, he began to cry out and said, "Jesus, thou son of David, have mercy on me." Some of the men tried to silence him, telling him that Jesus was very busy and could not be bothered with him at that moment, and saying for him to hold his peace. But instead of silencing him, he cried louder and louder, until Jesus heard him, stood still and commanded them to bring the man to Him.

The men who went to bring him told him to be of good comfort because the man, Jesus had asked for him. Bartimaeus hurriedly threw off the blanket that he had wrapped around himself, because it was a chilly day, stood up, and reaching out, took the arm of the man who stood closer to him and said, "I am ready! Please take me to Jesus!"

When they had reached Jesus, He asked him, "What wilt thou that I should do unto thee?" The blind man said to him, "Lord, that I may receive my sight." Jesus said to him, "Go thy way; thy faith has made thee whole!" Immediately the blind man had received his sight and began running and jumping and shouting and praising God, as he followed Jesus on down the highway.

Jesus, had on many occasions, cast out devils from the poor people who were possessed by demons. One woman comes to mind because she later became a loyal follower of Jesus, as well as a dear friend to me. Mary Magdalene was her name, and she was brought to Him for being accused of both being possessed by demons and of being found at times with the prostitutes. Jesus was said to have cast seven demons out of her and of the prostitute accusations I am not sure. I only know, however, that from that moment on, Mary lived a godly life and followed and worshiped Jesus as her Lord and Savior, as I, his earthly mother did. We became friends almost instantly and began to spend a lot of time together, both following Jesus and ministering to Him, His disciples, and anyone in the crowd who needed our help. In the evenings, when we were near the River of Jordan, we would set up our camp, and after we had fed everyone and cleaned up, Mary and I would take long walks by the water's edge and talk for a couple of hours. One evening after having preached and performed miracles for the multitude all day, Jesus stood and looked out into the crowd; He said to the Jews who believed on Him, these exact words:

"If ye continue in my word, then ye are my disciples indeed; and ye shall know the truth, and the truth shall set you free. Verily, verily, I say to you, whosoever committeth sin is the servant of sin and the servant abideth not in the house forever; but the Son abideth ever, if the Son, therefore, shall make you free, ye shall be free indeed" (John 8:34-36).

The Pharisees who were standing with the multitude became angry with Him for saying these things and from that day forward were always making false accusations. Their hatred of Jesus kept growing as His ministry continued.

A dumb man who was possessed with a devil was brought to Him. He cast the devil out and the man began to speak. The Pharisees then said that he cast out demons through the power of Satan. They began to accuse Him of blasphemy, called Him a devil and decided to find a way to take His life. They did and said everything they could think of, to put doubt in the minds of the people so that they would stop following Him, but, only God could control the peoples' hearts.

Jesus continued to heal many people. Not only did He open the eyes of the blind, make the deaf to hear, the lame to walk, and the dumb to talk, and he also healed many lepers. One of them who comes to mind is the leper who was named Simon. The poor man was full of leprosy to the point that he could not cover Himself to keep it from showing. He had been shunned by everyone because leprosy was very contagious. If he would even try to go out in public, the people would throw stones at him, and he would run for his life away from them.

He had been hiding in some bushes and was watching the multitudes with Jesus. As he was hiding and watching them, he saw that Jesus had turned and was walking toward him. He ran out of the bushes to Him and fell on his face, said, "Lord, will thou please make me clean?" Jesus said, "I will!" and then immediately the leprosy was gone, and the man was made clean. After this, Jesus's fame had spread throughout the land and great multitudes came together to both hear Him preach and teach, and to be healed of their infirmities.

One day, while Jesus was ministering and healing in a large house, a man was brought to Him to be healed of palsy. He wanted to be lain at the feet of Jesus, but the crowd was too large for them to get into Him. Some of the men went up on top of the house and with ropes tied to the man's bed, let him down through the roof; in the midst of Jesus. Seeing the faith of this man, Jesus told him to take up his bed and to rise and walk. The man did so and left running and jumping down the road glorifying God. His shouting as loud as he could, "Praise the Lord God of Israel, and thank you, God, Hallelujah" could be heard long after he had disappeared. Immediately, having had experienced the "healing power of Jesus," everyone whom Jesus had healed, realized who He was.

Jesus had been preaching, teaching, and healing the sick most of the day. It was getting late in the evening. No one had thought to bring food except for one little boy, whose mother had sent him with a small lunch. She had wrapped up for him some leftover fish and bread that the family had for the evening meal the night before. There were five barley loaves and two little fishes.

The disciples came to Jesus and told Him that the people needed to be sent on their way because they were getting hungry. Jesus refused to send them off; He told the disciples to have the men to sit down and bring the lad and his food to Him. He said that they would feed the crowd. The disciples were confused and said, "How can we possibly feed all these people with this meager amount of food? There are at least five thousand men, not to mention how many women and children that are with them."

When everyone was seated, Jesus took the loaves of bread and looking up to heaven, gave thanks to His Father. Breaking the bread, he then distributed it among the disciples.

The disciples then passed out the bread among the multitude, the men first and then the women and children. Likewise, He also took the fishes and gave thanks to His Father and the disciples distributed them as well. When everyone had eaten his fill after the meal was over, Jesus commanded the disciples to gather up the food that was left. They filled twelve large baskets with the fragments of barley loaves and fishes so that not a morsel was wasted. The people were all amazed at what they just had seen.

A few weeks later, Jesus again fed a large multitude of four thousand men, plus women and children, blessing only seven loaves of bread and a few little fishes. He always made sure that his followers were fed. Jesus never turned away the hungry, neither for natural food nor a spiritual "feeding for their souls!"

I have seen Jesus heal thousands of people. Every time that He healed them, He always told them that it was their faith that made them whole. His fame was growing and spreading throughout the countryside; multitudes were repenting and believing in Him and knowing that He was the Christ. The many others who did not believe in Him hated Him so badly that they were plotting and seeking a way to silence Him.

We had friends who lived in Bethany, a little village just outside of Jerusalem. The names of our friends were Lazarus and his two sisters, Mary and Martha. Jesus and I loved them very much. The sisters had sent for Jesus to come to their home as quickly as possible because His friend and their brother Lazarus had become very sick and the two women had been told that he was dying.

Jesus just seemed to be in no hurry at all to go to him. The disciples kept after Him for two days, begging Him to get started to their home. Jesus told them that Lazarus had already died and that He was taking His time so that His Father could be glorified. They did not understand, but nevertheless, they decided to step back and let Him handle the situation. They knew that He would go to His friend in His time, and that is just what He did.

Finally, Jesus said that it was time for them to go to Bethany to the home of His friend, Lazarus. By the time that He had arrived at Lazarus's home, his friend had been dead for four days and was in his tomb that had already sealed with a large stone in the doorway. As Jesus and the disciples approached the home, Martha, his older sister ran down the road to meet Jesus.

"Lord, you should have been here sooner and, Lazarus would not have died," she cried, falling at Jesus's feet. Then Jesus took Martha's shoulders and raised her up to Him and said, "Thy brother shall live again."

"Yes, my Lord, I know he will live again in the resurrection."

Then Jesus said to her, "I am the Resurrection and the Life: He that believeth in me, though he were dead, yet shall he live: Do you believe this Martha? He is going to live again."

"Yes, Lord," she said, "I believe that you are the Christ, the Son of God and I know that he will live again in the resurrection; but I only wish that you had come sooner and he would be alive now!"

The two sisters were a bit upset with Jesus for His not coming right away, but they knew that He had a very good reason for being four days late, and He would soon let them know. Then Martha went into the house and told Mary that Jesus was asking for her.

She ran out to him and told him also the same words that her sister Martha had said, that if he had been there earlier, Lazarus would not have died.

Jesus saw the sisters weeping and all their friends sobbing with them, and He too began to weep. "Where did you bury him?" He asked.

"Come and see, Lord!" they both said as they were walking Him to the grave. When they reached the tomb, Jesus said, "Remove the stone!"

"Oh no, Lord, you must not! Please!" cried Martha. "The body has begun to decay and the stench will be unbearable and it will make everyone sick. You know that Lazarus has been dead for four days, Lord!"

Not knowing what Jesus had planned to do to show the power of God, that others would believe, many of the people who had come to comfort Mary and Martha, and to mourn with them said that He was being very cruel to the sisters. They were beginning to become a little upset with Him.

"Remove the stone," Jesus commanded some of the men again and as they removed the stone. Jesus turning to the crowd, said aloud, "So that all of you may believe and it will glorify my Father!" and then turning back toward the tomb, He called out in a deep, loud voice so that the whole multitude would hear. "LAZARUS! Come forth." Then Lazarus appeared from out of the tomb, bound head and feet in his grave clothes and was standing before the amazed crowd, very much alive.

Jesus told them to loosen him, and they did. Then the whole multitude gave Father God the praise, honor, and glory and thanked Him for raising their loved one from the dead.

Everyone was in awe of what they had just seen and that day, even the nonbelievers also believed on Him.

Now the Pharisees became very worried because they feared that all the people will now believe on Jesus and that they may even make Him their king and this would indeed cause a lot of trouble with the Roman Government. From that day forth, they took counsel together, plotting to put Him to death.

Yes, raising Lazarus from the dead was indeed one of the greatest and most memorable miracles of them all. I always rejoiced in my heart because I knew that the Son of God was doing what He was sent to the earth to do: Teach love, to heal, to forgive sins, and most important of all, to save the whole world. And like John, the beloved disciple would write years later:

Taken from the "King James Version" of the Holy Bible.

"For God so loved the world, that he gave his only Begotten Son that whosoever believeth in him should not perish, but have everlasting life" (John 3:16).

Chapter 11

The Parables

Many times, during Jesus's ministry, He would teach in parables. He would tell a story using real people and real circumstances to explain different passages of the Scriptures. to get His point across that otherwise the people would not understand. The parable was a comparison of two things: most likely one good and the other one evil or in another sense—one right and the other one wrong. They always ended with a good moral, spiritual lesson.

One of His most memorial parables came about because He was explaining to the people why that everyone who called His name would not enter heaven. He was trying to tell them that they must believe and had to do the will of His Father. He said, "You will know men by their fruits. A good tree cannot bring forth evil fruit neither can a corrupt tree bring forth good fruit."

He said that He would compare the men who heard His preaching, and did what He had told them to be the "straight and narrow" way and those men would remind Him of a wise man. The wise man built his house upon a rock, and when the winds and the floods came, it did not fall because it was founded upon a rock. It had a good solid and dependable foundation.

The men who did not believe and did not do His sayings, to do the will of His Father reminded Him of a foolish man. The foolish man built his house on the sand. When the floods and the winds came, the house fell and was destroyed. Great was the Loss. Then another time when Jesus was preaching and teaching; there were many publicans and sinners who came to hear Him. The Pharisees who were over the Jewish people's laws and their religion, and some of the scribes were murmuring to themselves making scornful accusations because He could be found sitting, talking, or even eating with the sinners. They said that He could always be found with them. When He had heard their grumbling and complaining, He spoke this parable to them.

He said that He would tell them a story about a little lost sheep. Of course, everyone wanted to hear the story because many of them had tended sheep. He told the multitude that all sheep herders would know their sheep. If a shepherd has one hundred sheep and one is lost and is not numbered among the fold, he will leave the ninety-nine and go to find that one that is lost. When he finds it, he will throw it over his shoulders and call everybody and tell them that which was lost has been found. Then He told them that there is more joy in heaven over one sinner's repenting than over ninety and nine righteous people who need no repentance.

In another sermon, He was trying to show the people just how much that He and His Father loved them and how if they would repent and accept Him, they would not be lost. He began to tell them about a woman who had ten pieces of silver and had lost one coin. Losing only one piece, she hurriedly lit a candle and began sweeping the house and diligently searching until she had found the lost coin. Then she called all her friends and told them to rejoice with her because she had found the piece that she had lost. And again, Jesus said, "Likewise, I say unto you, there is joy in the presence of the angels of God over one sinner who repenteth."

Early one evening, Jesus went out and sat by the seaside, and when the multitudes came out to hear Him, He stepped up into a ship that was docked nearby and began to preach to them from the ship while they stood on the shore. He spoke to them in many parables that day and here are a couple of them that stand out in my mind.

He told them the parable of the sower: When the man went out to sow, some of the seeds that he had in his sack fell along the wayside. The birds came along and ate all of them. Yet some of the seeds that the man had in his sack fell into the rocks and the gravels where there was very little soil. Although they sprung up, they weren't well rooted, and when the sun came out, the small plants were scorched and wilted away. Another part of the seeds fell into the thorns, and the thorns choked them out. Finally, the remaining seeds fell into the good soil and brought forth a good crop. The disciples asked Him why He had spoken in parables and to explain the meaning of the Parable of the Sower, and He told them that He was trying to show the people some of the mysteries of the Kingdom of Heaven and then He began to explain the parable.

The seeds that fell by the wayside and were eaten by the birds are the people who hear the Word of the Lord and do not understand it and then Satan comes to them and causes them to forget what was sown into their hearts. The seeds that fell in stony places are the people who hear the Word of the Lord, and for a short time joys in it and then when tribulation or persecution arise are offended by the word. The seeds that fell into the thorns are the people who hear the Word of the Lord but the cares of the world choke out the word, and they are unfruitful. Now the seeds that fell on the good ground are the people who hear the Word of the Lord, comprehend it, and live by it, and bring forth good fruit a hundredfold. They stay strong in the word and are well rooted.

There was yet another parable of a sower. Jesus told them that the kingdom was like a man who sowed good seed in his field, and while he was asleep, his enemy sneaked in and sowed tares among the wheat, but when the wheat came up, the tares would come up also. Then the servants wanted to go out and gather the tares away from the wheat but the sower said, "No, let them grow together. If you try to gather up the tares before it is time to harvest the crop, then you shall also pull some of the good up by the roots destroying the good wheat." When the disciples asked for an explanation of this parable, He turned to them and, He said these words: "He that sowed the good seed is the Son of man, the field is the, and the good seed are His children, but the tares are the children of the wicked one. The enemy that sowed them is the devil the harvest is the end of the world, and the reapers are the angels. The angels shall gather them that do iniquity and cast them into a furnace of fire and then shall the Righteous shine forth as the sun in the kingdom of their Father."

He then asked the disciples if they had understood these sayings, and they said, "Yes, Lord, we surely do."

That same day, Jesus told the multitude about a true experience that He had a few days earlier and made it into a parable about a poor widow. He was in the temple, sitting near the treasury, a group of large wooden chests where the people would come and drop in their money contributions. He had been watching for quite a while as each person would walk by and throw his money into the collections. The rich tossed in much and just walked by not caring what they had put in because they would not miss the abundance of their contributions, although some of them still were maybe begrudging them. A poor widow walked by and reaching into her bag, and fumbling for the last two mites she had, she threw (about half a penny) them into the chest and walked away with a smile. She had given from her heart. He called the disciples over to Him and then continuing His sermon said these words: "Verily I say unto you, that this poor widow hath cast more in, than all they which have cast into the treasury: for all they did cast in of their abundance; but she of her want, she did cast in all that she had, even all her living." Jesus was simply telling them that the poor widow gave her, "all." He had said that the one who gives his "all" to the Father is blessed beyond measure and lives life more abundantly.

Then Jesus confused the disciples. He said to them these words: "Come, ye blessed of my Father and inherit the kingdom prepared for you from the foundation of the world. For I was hungry; and ye gave me meat. I was thirsty, and ye gave me drink. I was a stranger, and ye took me in. I was naked and ye clothed me. I was sick, and ye visited me. I was in prison, and ye came unto me."

The disciples began to ask Him when all these things had come to pass. They could not understand what He had said because they were talking among themselves and could not remember any time that they had found Him to be hungry, thirsty, naked, sick, or in prison. Then He stood up and looking at all of them, He said, "In as much as ye have done these things to the least of my brethren, ye have done it unto me," and again, they remembered that he had said many times before, "to do unto other as you would have them to do unto you!"

One of the last parables that I remember hearing Him teach was about the bridegroom and the ten virgins. The ten virgins took their lamps and went to meet the bridegroom. Now, five of the virgins were wise, and five of them were foolish. The five who were foolish took their lamps and took no extra oil with them, but the five who were wise took extra oil in their vessels with their lamps. While the husband-to-be busied himself with his errands, the virgins slumbered and slept. At midnight, there was a cry that their betrothed was coming and that they should go out to meet him. Then all ten of the virgins arose and trimmed their lamps. The foolish virgins said to the wise, "Give us some of your oil because our lamps have gone out." The wise virgins told them no because "then we would not have enough for ourselves. Go into town and buy some oil for yourselves."

While the foolish virgins were gone to buy more oil, the bridegroom came and the five wise virgins who were ready went into the marriage with their intended husband and the door was shut. When the foolish virgins came to the door and begged the Lord to open it, He said to them, "Sorry, I never knew you!"

Jesus then said to the multitude, "You must watch and be ready, for you know not the day or the hour that the Son of Man will come for you! The foolish shall go into everlasting punishment, but the righteous shall go into eternal life with the Father!"

There were so many parables that no one can remember them all, but all of them taught a great moral lesson, and the multitudes were able to learn the meaning of the kingdom and the "way." Jesus had preached to them that: "Everlasting life with Him and the Father was so easy to obtain; all they had to do was to believe and then to repent!

"Jesus is the truth and the life! Jesus is the only way into Heaven!"

Chapter 12

The Arrest

I remember the night before Jesus was arrested I couldn't sleep. I tossed and turned all night. I had a big lump in my throat, and I just had a terrible feeling that something horrible was going to happen. All throughout the next day, as I went about doing my usual chores, my heart was heavy. I could barely keep myself from crying. I was terribly upset, just a bit frightened and tired.

Late that evening right before sunset, John came barging into my house. Always being respectful of me, he had never just burst in before into my home without knocking and calling out to me. But this evening was different because he just threw open the door and almost ran inside. He had a look of horror on his face, and his eyes were swollen almost shut from his crying so hard. He came over to the chair where I was sitting, fell on his knees beside me, put one a hand on each of my shoulders and said with tears streaming down his face, "Mother Mary (all of the twelve that Jesus had called addressed me in this way), they have taken Jesus! They have taken our Lord! They dragged Him away!"

I stood up at that moment and in great astonishment, and fear, I said, "John, what in the world are you trying to tell me? Who has taken Jesus, who has taken my "son," and where, and why have they taken Him? How do you know this? What is happening?"

He said, "Oh, Mother Mary, they have arrested Him! The Jews, His people, have taken Him! The captain and soldiers of the high priest and they will probably kill Him this time, I just know it! We had gone with him, Peter, James, and me to the Garden of Gethsemane to pray, as we often do in the afternoons. You see, we were right there when it happened. I know because I saw them arrest Him! They were shoving Him and pushing Him and even knocked Him to the ground! One man spit in His face, and another man slapped across His mouth. They treated Him worse than they do hardened criminals!"

I had never seen John like this; he was hysterical. Handing him a cup of water, I told him to sit down and calm down so that he could tell me what had happened. As he began to compose himself, he then proceeded to tell me the terribly brutal story. The mob had quietly sneaked by the disciples because they had stopped a few yards up the path from where Jesus had gone to pray and were asleep. He told me how they had arrested Him and all the events as they had taken place from the beginning and everything that had happened throughout the day.

A couple of days before the Feast of the Passover, the chief priests and scribes had assembled at the palace of the high priest, Caiaphas. They were planning to arrest Jesus and then to have Him killed. But as Caiaphas had said, they could not do it on the feast day because it would probably cause a big riot among the Jewish people.

About the same time, Jesus was at the house of Simon the Leper whom He had healed of leprosy. While He was there, a woman came to Him carrying a small alabaster box of very precious expensive ointment and poured it over His head.

The disciples were aggravated with her for wasting the costly oil. Jesus said that she did it in preparation for his burial and told them in no way to rebuke her. At that moment, they did not exactly understand what He was saying to them, but they did not say anything else.

Earlier that day, Judas Iscariot, one of the His twelve trusted and beloved disciples had gone to the assembly of priests and scribes and asked them: "Just how much money would you pay me to deliver Jesus of Nazareth, the blasphemer, and liar into your hands?" They bargained with him settling on "thirty pieces of silver."

Having been told by Jesus to take care of the preparations of the Passover Feast, the disciples had made everything ready. Jesus sat down with the twelve men and as they ate, He said to them, "One of you who is sitting here with me this night shall betray me." Each one, in turn, began to say, "Is it I, Lord, is it I?"

He said these words: "It is one of the twelve that dippeth his hand with me in the dish, the same shall betray me. But woe to that man by whom the Son of man is betrayed! Good were it for that man, if he had never been born" (Mark 14:20, 21 KJV).

When He had dipped into the dish, He gave it to Judas Iscariot, the son of Simon, and then immediately Satan entered his body. Then Jesus said to him, "That thou doest do it quickly!"

Now no man at the table knew or understood what Jesus had said, and they all thought that He was sending Judas to buy provisions for them because he was carrying the purse that he kept their money in, and he was the treasurer for the group. He went away, and the disciples and Jesus finished their meal. The meal was bread and wine.

Jesus took a loaf of bread, and He broke it and giving each of the disciples a piece of bread, He said, "Take and eat, this bread represents my body that will be broken for you." They did eat, but they did not fully understand what was being done and what He was trying to tell them. Then He poured the wine into a cup. He passed it to the disciple sitting next to Him and said, "Drink, this is my blood which I will shed for the forgiveness of sin." Each one of them took a sip of wine.

Immediately after the meal was over, Jesus rose from the table, and laying aside His garments, He took a towel and wrapped it around Himself. He poured water into a large bowl and carried it over to the table. He then began to wash the feet of each of the disciples. Peter sat quietly watching Him. When it became his turn, and Jesus came to him, he refused to let His Lord bow down before him because he said that he felt unworthy. Jesus then looked at Peter and said these words to him, "If I wash thee not, thou hast no part with me."

Then Peter said to Him, "Lord, not my feet only, but also my hands and my head." Jesus then washed Peter's feet. Afterward, He told the disciples that they should be meek and lowly enough to also cleanse anyone's feet. He said that they called Him Lord and Master and He had done this as an example of humbleness to them.

Later that evening, Jesus had taken a few of His disciples, Peter, James, and John with Him when He had decided to go into the Garden of Gethsemane to pray. They had gone there several times because it was out of the way and they could have some privacy. They had stopped and talked a few minutes and then Jesus had left them a few yards down the road. He had gone up alone to the main part of the Garden to His big rock, where He always loved to kneel to talk to His Father. It was an altar for Him.

He came back and found that the disciples whom He had left behind had fallen asleep. Waking them up, He had asked them not to sleep, but to stay down there and pray as He went back up to the rock to pray alone. He had gone to them three times and each time, He had found them to be asleep. The third time, He told them to go ahead and sleep because it had come time for Him to be betrayed into the hands of the sinners.

At first, He had seemed to be a bit agitated with them because they could not stay awake and pray with Him, but seeing that they were so tired, He went back alone and left them to sleep and rest.

Suddenly, there was a lot of loud racket, and it had awakened the sleeping disciples. A huge crowd had sneaked by them and gone up the path and gathered where Jesus had gone to pray, and everyone was shouting and the three disciples could neither hear, nor understand anything that was being said. Standing back in the crowd, they did, however, learn that one of their members of His chosen twelve disciples, Judas Iscariot was indeed a traitor.

None of the other disciples had known that he had gone to the high priest a day before and had asked if the Jews would pay him money to betray Jesus to them. They did not know that he had asked for and was gladly given thirty pieces of silver to do this evil deed. He who had walked with Jesus for over three years and had seen firsthand the many amazing things that He had done. The miraculous healings of the sick, maimed, crippled, blind, deaf, and dumb, even casting out demons and raising people up from the dead, and still, he wanted to betray this man. What manner of man could he be?

He had told the high priest and his captain that whomsoever he should kiss that would be the man called Jesus, and they should take Him and lead Him away safely. We just can't believe that Judas knew at the time of his betraying Jesus, that the men were planning to have him killed.

Walking toward Jesus with a big smile on his face, Judas leaned over to Him and kissed Him on the cheek. "Hail, Master!" he said.

Jesus said, "Oh, friend, you betray me with a kiss?"

Then there was a slight scuffle and during that time, one of the disciples, Peter had reached out and grabbed one of the men's swords out of his sheath and cut off the ear of one of the servants of the high priest. Jesus screamed for them to stop, and picking up the man's ear, He blessed it and put it back in its place on the side of his head. The name of the man whose ear that Jesus restored to him was Malchus.

Then He said to Peter, "Peter, I tell you that those who live by the sword shall die by the sword."

And turning to the mob, He asked them why they were treating Him like a criminal when they had been with Him daily in the temple teaching, and they didn't take Him then. He had been in the homes of some of them and had eaten meals with them, and they didn't take Him then. Why now were they coming out against Him, as if He were a thief or a murderer, carrying staves and swords, but as He had said, the scriptures had to be fulfilled.

They bound His hands and drug Him off to see Annas, who was the father-in-law of the high priest, Caiaphas. Caiaphas felt that if he could rid the land of Jesus, the trouble with the Jews and the Romans would settle down and prevent the rebellion that he was expecting to take place at any time now. He knew that the Zealot leader, Barabbas, who had committed murder many times, had already been arrested and was in prison. Caiaphas thought that if he could somehow cause the deaths of both men, it should bring about, hopefully for him, not only a lot of recognition but also it would look to the Romans as if the Jews were doing everything that they could to keep the peace.

My heart sank in my chest. The lump in my throat almost choked me. In fact, I coughed myself to tears. I knew that the time for my son to get His Glory and the Glory of His Father had come! I loved Him so much. I had always known for thirty-three and a third years, Who He was, but my being a human mother, I wasn't sure how I was going to be able to live through this ordeal if the Father didn't intervene quickly.

"Oh, Father God, please give me strength," I begged. I thought that my heart would surely burst. I said to John, almost yelling. "Somehow I have to get to Him! Please, John, I have got to get to Him! Please take me to Him! Can we go to Him right now? Is there anything that we can do to help Him? Do you have any idea what they plan to do with Him?"

John took me to the area where the assembly of the elders, priests, and Caiaphas, the high priest, and a very large crowd had gathered. Most of the disciples had fled because they feared for their lives. I saw that Peter was still near, but he was standing toward the back of the huge crowd. I tried to get closer to see what they were doing to my "son." Many were there who had heard Jesus preaching and teaching. Some of them had recognized me, but I didn't care because I was there for "my son"; however, I knew in my heart that now, He was quickly becoming, "God's Son." I loved Him even more than I had realized.

Tears began streaming down my face, I could not control them, I could taste the salt, and I was to the point that I could barely see. I tried to compose myself until I could find out more about what was happening. I stood for hours, it seemed, and then arguing back and forth, the men decided that they should take Him before Pilate. I was so frightened that I wanted to scream. I thought if I could only awaken from this horrible nightmare, but I knew that I was not asleep.

I remember that I was not scared at all for myself, but I was so very scared for my "son" because I knew that His life was really in jeopardy. I also knew that if the Lord God, Jehovah, Himself, did not intervene and stop them very soon, that they would kill Him, they had tried before and failed. It had never gone as far as it was going this day, because He had never actually been arrested. I could not remember the crowd of people who were bringing accusations against Him, having ever been as large as it seemed to be now or as angry toward Him.

From time to time during His teachings, a few of the Pharisees who had mingled with His multitude of close, loyal followers, would stand up and shout a few obscenities at Him trying to disturb His meetings and His preaching, but then they would be gone as quickly as they had come. Today it seemed that no one was leaving, and they were bringing all kinds of ridiculous accusations against Him. They were calling Him a traitor, a liar, a crazy prophet, and were also accusing Him of blasphemy. They were planning to kill Him for no reason at all, just like they had killed poor John, who they had called "The Baptist."

Then I began asking John, the disciple of Jesus, a lot of questions that he really could not answer right at that moment. "John, please tell me, from where did this huge group of people come, and why do they hate Him so badly, and what exactly do they think he has done? Whose idea was this to arrest Him, the man who had only treated everyone with love? John, please help me to see what is happening and why. I am afraid that we will not be able to help Him this time. The crowd has too much control!"

Poor John tried to console me. He told me that all we could do was to wait and see how Pilate felt about Jesus. He said that he would have the final say, but he thought him to be a fair man.

The outraged mob began dragging Him to see Pilate, to have Him judged and to have a "mock" trial because they had already decided that he was guilty of all the crimes that they were falsely accusing Him of committing and all they wanted was to see Him dead. They did not care what they had to do to get this accomplished, because it was easy to see that their malicious hatred for Him was becoming more and more intense. I followed them and stayed back so that they would not notice that I was still there. Being His earthly mother, I could not bear to leave my "son" to "be eaten by the ravenous wolves"! He had not said a word in His own defense. I kept begging God, His heavenly Father, to stop this mockery, but I felt that I could not pray for anything except for Him to give me strength and courage.

I could see that the hatred of the crowd was becoming more and more dangerous and they were demanding the death penalty for the punishment of an innocent man. I was hoping and praying that this was not in God's plan but I knew that it had to be fulfilled as He had planned from the beginning. As they dragged Him to Governor Pontius Pilate's Hall of Punishment, I thought that my heart would surely stop beating at any moment and I longed to die soon of my broken heart.

Chapter 13

The Mock Trial

It is a hard thing to witness the barbaric beating almost to death of a hardened criminal who would be either a thief or a murderer, or even both and guilty many times over. But for a person, especially His "mother" to have to stand and watch a man be punished this way, who had never done harm to anyone, neither physically nor emotionally, was almost impossible to have to do. I did, and I just stood right there through it all! I could not, and I would not leave His side because He had already been betrayed by someone whom He had loved. I, His mother, would not let Him be betrayed again, at least not by me. It has now been several weeks since that horrendous ordeal, but I can remember the mock trial as if it had just ended this morning.

Pontius Pilate, the governor of Judea, had appointed to the office of high priest of the Jews, a man who was called Annas. Now it was Annas who had sent his son-in-law, Caiaphas, and his officers to arrest Jesus in the Garden of Gethsemane and had told them to bring Him to his court. After questioning Him and getting no answers that satisfied him, the angry Caiaphas, along with his officers and his band of followers decided to take Jesus to Governor Pilate's Judgment Hall. Although the high priest had the authority to make an arrest, he did not have the power to condemn his prisoner to death. That was only the governor's right to do so.

Arriving at Pilate's Judgment Hall, the band met him coming out to them. They told him that they had arrested a blasphemer, a liar, and a traitor to Caesar. Pilate told them that he wanted to talk to Jesus alone. He took Him down one of the corridors and into a large room in the palace. The two of them were gone for over an hour. Finally, they returned to face the crowd. They walked out; Jesus was in the lead of course, because He was the prisoner, and His hands were still bound in front of Him.

Pilate stepped up on a raised platform in the hall. He began to tell the crowd that he had questioned Jesus and he could not find any evidence that He had committed any crime. He said that in his opinion, Jesus was innocent of all the charges that they had brought against Him, and therefore, He should be set free. He stated that if they insisted on His being arrested that they would have to take Him before King Herod in Galilee. Herod had been appointed to his kingdom by the Roman Emperor Augustus Caesar.

Caiaphas bowed toward Pilate and then motioned for his captain and the officers to take Jesus to Herod's palace. When they reached the palace, he explained to King Herod the situation and told him what the Jews were hoping to accomplish with Jesus having been arrested. After talking with them for a few minutes, Herod was not certain what he should do with Jesus. He immediately insisted, as did Pilate, that he wanted to speak with Him alone.

He tried to get Him to do something that would prove that He was some kind of god like He had been claiming to be. Jesus refused to answer any of Herod's ridiculous questions or to play any of his childish games. Being somewhat angry, King Herod told Caiaphas that he would not make any decisions concerning His punishment and all he could do, was to send Him back to Pilate's hall. He told them that he would let Pilate be responsible for the judgment in the case against this so-called self-proclaimed King of the Jews because he did not have time for such foolishness. From there, it was just back and forth, with the two rulers playing mind games because neither of them wanted to make the final ruling. They both had realized very early that the Jews would not be satisfied with anything less than a sentence of death for Jesus. Herod and Pilate knew that Jesus was an innocent man who had committed no crimes of any kind.

Pontius Pilate did not want to make the final judgment. He could not understand why the people hated Him so much to have arrested Him in the first place. He had heard of various miracles that Jesus had performed, even for some of the family members of the high priest's officers.

Another reason that the governor did not want to make any bad decisions for Jesus was that his wife had begged him not to take His life. She said that she had been having terrible nightmares about Him from the time that He had been arrested. She was afraid for her husband to do anything to harm the Man in any way. She had also said that He seemed different from anyone whom she had ever met.

Nevertheless, it had finally become time to make the final decision of what to do with the man Jesus, and it was Pilate's choice to rule on what was to be His fate.

I had been so hopeful since He had been arrested and was finally brought to Pilate's Hall, that He would be saved. It was the time of what we called the Governor's Feast and Pilate was to release one of the prisoners to the Jews. I just knew their choice would have to be Jesus and the reason was very clear:

The only other prisoner at the time was a zealot named Barabbas. This man was a notorious thief, a cold-hearted murderer, a rapist, had started many riots, and was against any part of the Roman rule. He had led a band of cutthroats for several months before being arrested. He was so demonic that he would cut a man's throat just because he looked him in the eye and then would leave his dead body on the side of the road to rot. How could the crowd possibly choose this Barabbas over a man who was as compassionate and as loving as Jesus?

I just could not believe that these "people," the very people who had been a part of or their families had been a part of; the miracles that He had performed over the past three and one third years would choose such a cutthroat criminal over Him.

I stood up straight and on my tiptoes, when Pilate stepped out onto the platform again so that I could get a better view and to hear clearly every word that he said. Looking out into the large multitude, he asked, "Now tell me which prisoner you want me to release to you?"

It seemed that the entire crowd cried out in unison, "Barabbas! Barabbas! Give us Barabbas! We choose Barabbas!"

I thought my heart would burst, and I was going to choke to death when Pilate paused for a moment and then he asked, "What should I do with Jesus, who is called Christ, Your King? I tell you all that I find no fault in this man! I believe that He is innocent!"

Then the Jews cried out to him, telling him that if he let Him go that he was no friend of Caesar's and since Jesus had made Himself a king, then He had spoken against the emperor. Pilate asked them if they wanted him to crucify their king and they became angry with him and said that their only king was Caesar. Looking out into the crowd, he asked them again, "What would you have me to do I do with this man?" He knew that the choice was not his; because the whole crowd shouted in unison, "Crucify Him! Crucify Him! We want you to crucify Him!"

At that point, I felt my legs crumbling under me. Mary and John each grabbed one of my arms and held me up for a few minutes until I could get my balance and take a couple of deep breaths. Mary put her arms around my back so that I could lean on her. She had seemed to always be by my side ever since Jesus had cleansed her from the demons a couple of years before.

Suddenly, Pilate called for a bowl of water and a towel and standing before the crowd and dipping his hands into the water, he said, "I wash my hands of this. I am innocent of this man's blood! Take Him quickly, do as you will!"

He stopped for a minute and then He raised his right hand to silence the crowd. Then speaking in a loud, clear voice, he told the soldiers to take Jesus around to the whipping stocks and to scourge Him, thirty-nine licks less one. He was hoping that a hard beating would be enough to satisfy the angry mob.

Mary and I walked around the hall behind them, knowing all the while that what we were about to witness was going to be the most unthinkable act that we had ever had to watch. Again, I had to stay. I could not betray my "Son"! I was so scared for Him because I had heard how horrific crucifixions could be, and although I had never seen one, I could not bear the thought of His being crucified.

Normally, women were not allowed to watch this rigorous part of the cruel and barbaric punishment of the accused, but the soldiers seemed to be amused that His mother was there so Mary and I were permitted to stay. The soldiers thought that would be more heartache for Jesus to endure. I don't know if He had seen us there because we had tried to stay hidden from His view so it would not be more punishment for Him.

Jesus was pushed, knocked down to the ground, drug through gravels, kicked in the ribs, and then shoved headfirst right into the whipping post. The soldiers all were laughing and mocking Him. One of the men walked up to Him and spit right in His face. Another man slapped Him across the face with the palm of his hand and left a big red hand print on His right cheek. Then the soldier who stood closest to Him grabbed His hands and tied them to the post so tight that they were turning a reddish purple. Jesus never said a word or made any effort to resist any of them, no matter what they did. He stood there as meek as a newborn lamb.

It was so hard for me to watch "my" Jesus, who had never harmed anyone in His entire life, be treated this way. Especially my "son" and knowing who He was! I wanted to strike out at them and scream out at them, "Don't you know who this man is?" All I could do was stand quietly and watch, with tears running down my face. I felt as if my heart would burst right out of my chest. There was not one person, in the whole crowd, who stepped up to offer any help to Him in any way. The evil, cruel soldiers were laughing and enjoying His mock trial and torture so much.

I could not understand why His Father would allow these savage, monstrous men to treat Him so badly. I wanted to cry out to

Him and ask Him to stop this and make them know who He was. I had to keep silent because I knew better than anyone why He had come to earth and that His work here had to be finished just as He and His Father had planned. I was certain that although these cruel men thought that they had the authority given to them by Pontius Pilate to do what they were doing, it was only happening because Jesus, Himself was permitting it to be done so that it would glorify His Father in heaven.

Another soldier came over to Him and laughed sadistically, and for no reason at all, just reached up to His face and started ripping out handfuls of Jesus's beard by the roots and throwing it to the ground. His precious chafed face was beginning to bleed a little in places where the facial hair had been ripped out so roughly. By the time the soldier had finished, it almost looked as if Jesus had been clean shaven.

I turned to the side and caught a glimpse of poor Peter, one of the trusted disciples, whom Jesus loved dearly. Bless his heart, he was terrified for his life, but he just couldn't stay away completely, so he tried to hide out from the crowd. He had sworn an oath to Jesus earlier that he would not leave His side and would lay down his life for Him. Jesus had replied to him that before the cock had crowed that he, Peter, would have denied Him three times. Naturally being Peter, he had still put up a slight argument and would not admit that he could ever deny the Christ.

A small group of people had dug a short trench by the side of the path and had built a fire in it to try to warm themselves because the air was becoming quite chilly in the afternoon. Peter walked across the road to join them so that he could warm himself also. Almost everyone who had been standing around the Hall area had a blanket wrapped around Himself, except for Jesus of course. The soldiers had stripped Him down to a thin loincloth, and He was shivering and shaking from the cold. They didn't care, and one of the soldiers had found humor in the idea that the "King of the Jews" was standing out in the cold almost naked. He had turned to a fellow soldier and said,

"Hail, the shivering frozen king! He's a god too! Who would think that a god would get cold? Some joke, huh?"

Suddenly, one of the women who were standing next to the fire pointed at Peter and said, "That man, I remember seeing him with this Jesus! I believe that he may even be one of His twelve trusted disciples." Peter began cursing and swearing that he had no idea who the person that she was talking about could be. A few minutes later, a man on the other side of the fire recognized him as well. Peter kept denying the accusations and calling everyone crazy. He told them that they were mistaking Him for some other person who looked like him.

An older man stepped up to the fire, and standing next to Peter, he said, "I know for a fact that this man is a follower of Jesus and was with Him when we arrested Him in the garden. He is the man who had become angry with Annas and the band of officers who had come with Him. He was so full of wrath that he grabbed one of the officer's swords off his side and cut the man's right ear off, letting it fall to the ground. That man is a kinsman of mine. I tell you, I know this to be true. Pointing to the other side of the road, he said, "You can ask the man, his name is Malchus and he is standing right over there. Come with me, I will take you to him!"

Peter was becoming terrified for his life now because he had been recognized by three different people in only a matter of minutes, and he had denied that he had ever known Jesus three times. Suddenly, he heard the cock crow twice. Peter was beside himself; sobbing, he turned and ran down the road away from the crowd.

A few minutes later, a large, robust Roman soldier walked over to Jesus carrying what one of the men called a cat of nine tails. It was the most hideous-looking thing that I had ever seen. It was a rope whip with nine long thin pieces of leather knotted several times down each piece. At the bottom of each piece of leather, there was either a tiny piece of sharp metal or bone, so that they will dig into the body and drag out pieces of bloody flesh. Then the beating began. The whip made a switching sound each time it flew into His back and drug out bits and pieces of bloody flesh. Gasping at every blow, I could hardly breathe. Time just seem to have stopped, I could not bear to watch the scourging. Each time the soldier hit Him, I felt as if he were beating me. Jesus never cried out once, but He would only cringe at each blow. I stopped counting at number nineteen. I kept turning away and praying to the Father to please intervene and stop this senseless beating before the soldier had beaten Him to death. I would turn back toward Jesus because although I could not bear to watch; again, I could not desert my "son"! I knew that He was God in the flesh; no one could know this better than I. I also knew that He had felt every blow and the pain was the same pain and agony that any "human" would feel.

Still, from my human standpoint, he was my son also. I loved Him like any mother loves her child. I cleaned Him up when He was a small child and wiped His little runny nose when He had a cold. I held Him in my arms, many times when He would cry because His precious heart was broken because of something the cruel human race would do out of hatred and spite.

He had been so badly beaten, so torn and bloody, and so grotesquely disfigured that had I not followed Him from afar the entire time, I would not have recognized "my son"! The same baby whom I had carried in my womb, some thirty-three years earlier, and the same young boy that I had watched grow into a "God-Man" right before my eyes!

One of the men in the crowd standing nearest to Jesus grabbed a handkerchief out of his pocket and blindfolded Him. He then motioned for the man who was standing on the right side of Him to bash Him unmercifully in the face. He then took off the blindfold and told Jesus that since He was a god to prophesy to the crowd and tell them who had just hit him. Of course, Jesus never complied with their childish games.

A couple of the soldiers had found a scarlet robe and had put it on Him. One of the other cruel men had platted a crown of thorns. I am not sure where he had picked the thorns. I thought that they were taken from one of the lovely rosebushes that were in Pilate's beautiful garden or they were taken from the bramble bushes that grew all throughout the countryside.

Laughing and taunting Him, the soldiers began to have a mock coronation of the "King of the Jews." The man who had platted the crown then slapped it on His Jesus's head. He then hit it with a long reed as hard as he could. The blood spurted everywhere, running down in His eyes, across His face off His chin, and onto the robe. By this time, His face was so swollen and bruised that His eyes were almost shut and His mouth and nose were bleeding. It looked as if some of His intestines were hanging out holes that the whip had made in His back and side. There were parts of His bones showing through His ripped flesh. Then they put the reed in His right hand and bowed on one knee before Him and began mocking Him saying, "Hail, King of the Jews."

After they had had their fun, they removed the robe and began to drag Him back around in front of the Judgment Hall and back to Pilate. He was wearing the thin loincloth about His waist, and the crown of thorns still was on His precious head. Pilate raised his hand, and when he had lowered it, the soldiers took Jesus away to be crucified.

Mary, John, and I stayed back in the shadows hoping that Jesus would not know that we had witnessed the scourging and all of the mockery. Still, we could not bear to leave. Almost everyone had left Him but the soldiers and the priests and their officers. All the disciples except John had fled in fear of their lives. Peter came back a short while later.

I was beginning to wonder, just out of curiosity, where Judas had gone. By this time, I had heard about His betraying kiss and his payment of the thirty pieces of silver that he had been given for the betrayal. How could anyone walk with Jesus all that time and sell Him at any price? Then I asked John if he had seen or heard anything from Judas. A man in the crowd heard me ask the question and he began to describe to us what had happened to him after he had maliciously, betrayed Jesus to the Caiaphas and his men.

The man told us that Judas realizing what he had done, and seeing that Jesus had been condemned to die on the cross, repented himself and then he went to high priest and begged him to take back the thirty pieces of silver. He told him that he had sinned and had betrayed innocent blood. He wanted them to set Jesus free because he had realized that it was a terrible mistake and that they all would answer to God for this cruel act.

Caiaphas only laughed at him because the damage was already done and remarked that he did not care and there was no turning back. With a big, sneering smile, He said that he had worked for months to see this day come. Now he, Caiaphas, the chief priest, could claim the victory for ridding the kingdom of this troublemaker forever. He would possibly receive a great reward from the Roman Government and maybe even praises from Caesar himself.

Judas was so upset that he threw the money up into the air, and it landed all throughout the holy room of the temple. He ran down through the corridor and out into the yard. He then went outside of town and, finding a rope and a large tree, hanged himself.

Now the priests quickly picked up the thirty pieces of silver, but they said it would be unlawful for them to put it back into the treasury because it had been paid as the price of blood. They took council and decided to buy the potter's field, which they called the field of blood and there any stranger who dies and does not have a burial place of his own can be buried. It was said of Judas that it would have been better for him if he had not been born.

It is sad for a man to follow Jesus and then to turn his back on Him. He has condemned himself to walk down the lonely path to destruction. There is, however, a way to receive the forgiveness of a merciful Lord! All one must do is to repent and ask!

Chapter 14

The Crucifixion

I have suffered a loss this night. My "son" has been crucified. The pain in my heart is so intense because it has been broken into a million pieces. I feel as if it has been ripped right out of my chest. I have wept until there are no more tears. I do not know how I will make it throughout the rest of my life, without having my "son" here with me. He was my life.

Having watched the brutal cruelty and the barbaric punishment of an innocent man, I could only gasp for each breath that I took, thinking and yes, even hoping, that each one would be my last. I kept silently crying out to Father God, to please mercifully stop this execution of His Son and let the men realize what they were doing. However, as it progressed, I knew that this was, indeed, the reason that Jesus had come to this earth and the purpose must and was at that very moment being fulfilled.

I did not spend the time alone; however, John was trying to comfort me as Jesus had asked him from the cross to do. Mary stayed with me as well. They were both in mental anguish with me. But Jesus said that it would be three days, and we just had to wait. I did not know how I would make it through the next three days. But knowing that my God had seen me through so many trials already; I knew that He was not going to leave me now. He is merciful and true, and we had to put our trust in Him, more now than ever.

Mary and I prepared a meager meal for the disciples who all had gathered into try to comfort each other in our terrible grief. We were all remembering special moments from the horrendous event that we had just witnessed. To all of us, we had just seen an innocent man murdered right before our eyes.

I remember as I was standing and watching Jesus hanging on the cross in so much pain and agony that I saw a teardrop on the lashes of His right eye. I knew that the spikes and the ropes were not holding Him up there, as it always had the other people who had been crucified. It was the unconditional *"love"* that He had for the entire world. This crucifixion was for all who had lived in the past, the present, and who were going to be born to live in the future for many generations to come. Very few people who stood there in the crowd with me on crucifixion day had a clue of what was happening. To most of them, it was just another death on the cross. Sadly, for some of them, it was an exciting way to spend their time.

Most of the Roman soldiers, like Marcus for example, watching and participating in the cruelty was a kind of barbaric hobby. It was so sad to think that any man could honestly enjoy this day and have a wicked smile on his face as he watched. I felt sorry for them because they were missing out on an eternity in Heaven. I knew that as soon as they had taken their last breath, they would be like the rich man whom Jesus had taught about in one of His sermons. The man had died and then immediately, he had opened his eyes, in torments because he was too proud and too foolish to repent of his sins.

While the disciples, Mary, and I were just sitting around talking, John and Peter began remembering details about the crucifixion. Since most of the other disciples did not witness the dreadful event, they began to tell them some of the things as they had happened.

After the mock trial was over and all the soldiers and the other men had their fun, they decided that it was time for Jesus to be crucified.

The soldiers threw Him over to an old cross that they had built out of rough splintery lumber. They told Him that he had to pick it up and carry it all the way up Calvary Hill to the place of the crucifixion that was called Golgotha or "the skull." The heavy load would be more punishment for Jesus. Anyone in the past who had been crucified had to carry the extremely heavy crossbar part of the cross only. Jesus was made to carry His entire cross, which in His weakened condition, having lost so much blood, would have been impossible for a "normal man" to have done.

There were two other men who had been condemned to death. They were to be crucified at the same time with Jesus. The soldiers were going to hang Him on a cross in the middle of the two. One of them was a notorious thief, and the other one was a murderer.

Now everyone must realize that Jesus had lost a lot of blood. He had been badly beaten until His insides were hanging out. Having had his beard yanked out by the roots, He was still wearing the crown of thorns that had been slapped on His head and hit with a reed. He was nearly naked, and it was cold, and His feet were bruised and blistered from the long walk he had taken through the gravels, thorns, and thistles by the wayside. No one can imagine the agonizing pain that He was already suffering, and yet He was still going to be crucified. I wondered why they couldn't see that He had been punished enough.

Jesus was probably only halfway up the hill when He staggered with the heavy cross that he carried on His back and fell flat on His face. One of the soldiers being so angry and not intending to be of any help at all grabbed a man from out of the crowd whose name was Simon. He shoved him to the cross and told him to help Jesus carry it to the top of the Hill. You could see that the poor man's heart was broken because he had tears running down his pale, colorless face. He began to pick up the cross and lifted Jesus to stand. A few minutes after Simon had been helping Jesus, the color that he had lost came back into his face, his eyes had brightened and were shining, and he was smiling sweetly. John and I knew instantly that he had repented to Jesus and was now a righteous man. He was feeling the "power of God's Son" and had the peace that only a saved man could know.

Throughout, the horrendous torture that he endured, Jesus never once cried out from the pain. He did not ask His tormentors for mercy. I was so scared for my "son" because I could not imagine His having to take any more of their cruelty.

When Jesus, with the large crowd following behind Him finally reached the place of crucifixion, my stomach began to turn, and I became deathly ill. I saw that the two other men who had been condemned to death and were to be hanged on the cross with Him were already hanging on their crosses. Those two men were gasping for breath and were crying out in pain and anguish. There suffering was unbearable for them.

Two of the soldiers, who were both very huge men, walked over and took the cross from the backs of Jesus and Simon and threw it down on the ground. Then one of them shoved Simon, almost knocking him down and told him to get out of their way or they just might decide to crucify him as well. The other soldier threw Jesus down on the cross.

Each of them picked up an old, rusty spike, about, I would guess, at least four or five inches long, and yanked Jesus's arms and raised them up as far as they would go and stretched them out across the upper part of the cross. The large hammer that each of them held in his hand would have taken two smaller men even to lift it. As they raised the hammers, I felt myself gasping for air. I felt very weak at that moment, and my legs just went out from under me.

If John had not have been standing by my side to hold me, I would have fallen. I could not see them, but they each hammered the spike into His hands with one earth shattering thud, nailing them into both of His hands at the same moment. You could hear His flesh burst open as the spikes were driven into His hands. That gruesome sound of His tearing flesh will haunt me for the rest of my life. It is something that the mind and heart can never forget.

Then they were ready to nail His precious feet. They crossed one slightly over the other, and because they had more flesh to go through, they had to use a somewhat longer spike. It was at least seven inches long. Jesus just groaned a little bit as the spike went into His feet. I had to muffle my screams when I heard the ripping flesh. John and I weren't that close, but we still felt a few drops of His precious blood as it had splattered on our arms. Then about three of the men picked up the cross, with Jesus hanging on it, stood it upright, and then just let it drop into a big hole that one of them had dug earlier that day.

They pushed hands full of dirt and stones around it so that it would stand straight and not fall over. He was covered in His precious blood from His head to His feet. It was pouring from the crown of thorns on His head, from the old rusty spikes in His hands and out of His feet. The blood was dropping to the ground under the cross, and it had made a small round puddle around the bottom.

Governor Pilate had taken a large plank of wood and carved a sign that read:

JESUS OF NAZARETH THE KING OF THE JEWS

He handed it to one of the soldiers and told him to hang it up over Jesus's head because he wanted it to be seen by the entire crowd. Making sure that everyone there could read and comprehend His title, Pilate had it written in three languages: Hebrew, Greek, and Latin.

After the soldiers had crucified Jesus, they took His garments and ripped them into four parts, giving one to each soldier, and as it was written in the scriptures, they did cast lots. They were laughing and enjoying themselves.

When the crucifixion was over, there were only a few of us left standing near the cross, John, the disciple of Jesus, Mary Magdalene, and my sister, who had gone with me to try to help comfort me. They all loved Jesus almost as much as I did. He looked down at us, and He said these words, "Woman, behold thy son!" and then looking at John, He said, "Behold thy mother!" From that hour, I have been a part of John's home.

Then a couple of hours later, looking straight ahead, He said, "I thirst!" He had asked so meekly for a sip of water. The afternoon had warmed up quite a lot, and the sun was beginning to beam down on Him. He still had not made a sound. His whole being was stained with the shed crimson red blood that had dried in big crusted layers all over Him. Dirt and sand had been blown into His mutilated flesh from the gusts of wind throughout the day. I am sure that His wounds were burning, not to mention the flies and gnats biting Him and the sweat running all over Him. He was in so much pain. I could barely stand there and look at Him. His great suffering of body, heart, and mind showed in His face. It was tearing my heart out! He was so humble that He reminded me of an adorable, meek baby lamb. I thought there is no wonder that He has been called "The Lamb of God"!

One of the soldiers said, "Water, you want water? Okay, I will give you water." He laughed a hideous laugh that I have ever heard in my life, and then to my disbelief, he dipped a cloth in vinegar mingled with gall and put it on a sword and lifted it up to His mouth for Him to drink. Of course, He just spit it out. Sadly, the same cruel man had given the thief and the murderer who were hanging on either side of Him a cool drink of water. The Christ, God's Son, who had made the water for everyone to drink, was grossly refused even just a sip.

I can't count the times my heart was broken that day. They held me back. I wanted so badly to run to Him and say, "Son, please do not die for these people. They don't deserve your love, come down and let them see who you are and then they will see you in all your glory and then they will repent. You don't have to die!" I wanted Him to call the angels, and I knew He could call Gabriel. However, I also knew in my heart that He was glorifying His Heavenly Father, and I would not ask Him to do anything against the will that God had for Him from the day that He was conceived. He was not "my son" now, but He was God's son. I wiped the tears from my eyes and gave thanks to our Father God for His Son and allowing me to "have" Him as "my son" for a few years.

Then I heard one of the men who was hanging on the cross on the left side of Him say, "If you are who you say you are then, put an end to this torture! Come down and save us all three! If you are who you claim to be, then stop our suffering! Can you not call on your angels! You should have thousands of them! Do something, anything! Please, stop this pain!"

And the man who was hanging on the cross to His right said, "Do you not see that this man is innocent? We are both guilty of all charges and should be here but not this Man. Jesus, will you please remember me when you come into your kingdom?" Jesus then turned to the man so passionately and said, "Today, thou shalt be with me in paradise." I heard a few snickers throughout the crowd, but I knew that He had the almighty power to "keep His promise."

Then the chief priest also began mocking Him, saying, "Look at Him. He saved others, but Himself He can't save. If he is the King of Israel, let him now come down from the cross, and we will all believe and worship him." Then he said with a sneer, "He trusted in God. Let him deliver him now If he will have him because he has claimed that he is the son of God. Some son, if He is not lying, let Him prove His claim! Let us see His power!"

Shortly after their mocking Him, Jesus said, "It is finished!" and commended His spirit into the Father's hands and then He died. A few minutes later, the soldiers came to break the legs of the men who were hanging on the crosses because it was a custom to quickly end their lives after a long tiring day. Having their legs broken, they would quickly suffocate because they could not bear the excruciating pain of trying to raise themselves up to breathe. It was also an attempt to punish them one last time before they died.

Since Jesus had already died, and according to the Scriptures, that none of His bones would be broken, the soldiers did not even touch His legs. One soldier just had to be sure that He was dead, so he took his sword and pierced His side and let the remaining blood and water flow from His body. I thought I saw a few drops fall on him.

I don't remember much about the horrible earthquake, but I do know that suddenly, there was a loud clap of thunder. Lightning streaked through the sky and then it had darkened from the sixth hour until the ninth hour. It was very scary because you could not see your hand in front of your face. People, having been blinded by the darkness, were running around in circles. They were screaming and fearing for their lives. Suddenly the terrible earthquake came, and huge parts of buildings were falling, and big boulders were being blown across the way because of the horrible high winds. The scene was so horrifying because the earth was convulsing to the likes of which had never or will have ever been known. Some of the men said that the veil of the temple was ripped from the top to the bottom.

As I was standing there watching the confusion, I heard several of the people even the Centurion who had pierced Jesus's side with his sword say, "Surely, this Man is truly the 'Son of God'! What have we done this day? Oh! God, please, find it in your heart to forgive us!"

John took my hand and said, "Come, Mother Mary, let us go home now, and you can try to get some rest. We will come back later this evening after everyone is gone! We will spend some time alone with Jesus!" My "new" son, John, had already begun to take care of me as Jesus had asked him to do just before He had died. Father God is still blessing me beyond measure! He is still watching out for me as He did Joseph, Jesus, and I, while His Son, whom He had "loaned" to me, was growing into manhood, the past thirty-three and a third years.

Chapter 15

He Finally Came Down

The crucifixion is now over, and everyone has left. On Calvary's Hill, there are three dead men each hanging on a cross. One of them is a thief, one of them is a murderer, and the other man, the one who is hanging on the cross in the middle is the Son of God, who came down to the earth in human form to sacrifice Himself so that the whole world might be saved.

"For God so loved the world that he gave his only begotten Son, that whosoever believeth in him should not perish, but have everlasting life" (John 3:16).

John said to Mary and me that a rich man from Arimathea named Joseph went to Governor Pilate's palace and begged for the body of Jesus. Since the next day was the Sabbath and according to Jewish custom, all dead bodies had to be buried before the preparation was started, he asked for the body for burial. Because, he, too, was saddened by the crucifixion and felt that an innocent man had been killed, Pilate commanded that remains be delivered unto Joseph.

After leaving the governor's palace, Joseph had stopped at the home of a man named Nicodemus, who had planned to go to the cross with him to help take out the spikes that had been nailed in Jesus's hands and His feet. A few hours earlier, Nicodemus had purchased some pieces of fine white linen cloth and many spices, a mixture of myrrh and aloes, which would weigh about one hundred pounds, to take with them to the tomb so that they could bury Jesus in the tradition of the Jews.

John, Mary, and I went back to the cross to be near Jesus when "He finally came down." Mary and I stood back behind the cross so that we couldn't see the men taking the spikes out of His hands and His feet. We could hear the weird, squeaky, rippling sounds. It took them a few minutes because they were careful not to tear His hands and feet any more than the spikes had already torn them.

Two of them pulled out the spikes while the other one held His body up so that it would not fall and hit the ground. When they had removed the spikes and the taken the ropes off Him, they laid His body down at the bottom of the cross. I walked over to Him and lifted His lifeless upper body, His head and His shoulders over onto my lap, and held Him in my arms for a short time. He was such a bloody mess. My tears were falling so hard that they rinsed some of the precious blood off His face. The crown of thorns had fallen off His head as I lifted Him into my arms. I had intended to get it later so that I could break it into a million pieces but I forgot all about the ugly piece of pure mockery and torture.

I know that it may sound rather strange, but many times I have wondered about the whereabouts of the poor cruel man who platted the hideous crown of thorns and put it on Jesus's head. I wonder what became of him. I do hope that when the earth became dark, the big earthquake shook the earth and Jesus had died that the man realized who had worn his "masterpiece." I hope that he repented of his terrible deed.

I was also happy to hear that a few of the Roman soldiers and some of the officers of the High Priest Caiaphas had realized the truth and repented. However, I have never heard that Annas or Caiaphas ever saw the "light." It was a shame that their pride and stubbornness could send them to Hell. I do know, however, that Jesus was very pleased to forgive the ones who asked Him. All anyone must do to be forgiven is to simply ask Him.

While I was sitting there holding Jesus in my arms, John walked over to me and kneeling beside me, he lifted His body off my lap and gently turned him over to lie on the ground in front of the cross. He then took both of my hands and helping me to stand, he said, "Mother, Joseph, Nicodemus and I are going to take care of our Lord's body now. Let Mary take care of you while we are getting the body ready. She can minister to you, and maybe you can relax."

Then He called Mary to come over to us. She had been sitting a few yards from me because she knew that I needed a few last minutes of privacy to spend alone with my "son."

John asked her to take me to sit over on the other side of the road because he thought that my watching them prepare Jesus's body would be very upsetting for me. He told her to get me a cup of water and maybe try to help me to get a few minute's rest before we would leave to go to our homes.

Then he helped Joseph and Nicodemus wrap Jesus's lifeless body in the clean white linen after they had anointed Him with the expensive ointment. After the body was prepared for burial, the three men carefully lifted Him into a tiny one horse cart that Joseph had brought with him to carry the body to the tomb.

Joseph had carved a sepulcher out of the rock and made a type of small cave back in the hillside a few years earlier. Jesus was only borrowing the unused tomb for a little while and then it would be returned to Joseph and his family. We all knew that, in fact, it would be a short time, because we had heard Him say that in three days, He would be raised from the dead. We all knew that He was indeed the Son of God and that He would not and could not stay dead!

When we reached the tomb, Mary and I stood back to the side while the three men took the body down from the cart and carefully placed it inside. Then they had rolled a large stone in front of the tomb to seal it and to keep out wild animals. After they had finished all the preparations, we all said our goodbyes to each other, and John and Mary took me home.

When we reached the house, I walked in and over to my big soft chair that was sitting against the wall and sat down for it seemed hours. I had Jesus's precious blood all over me from when I was holding Him at the cross, and I just couldn't make myself wash it off right away. Finally, I went into another room and took a washbasin and poured some water into it and took a bath.

When I had finished, had dressed, and gone walked back into the room, I found that some of the others who had stayed with me had taken a blanket and found a place to lie down to try to get some sleep. We were all at John's house, me, the other disciples, and Mary Magdalene. We all wanted to stay together to comfort each other and to await the resurrection.

I went over to my chair to wipe out the blood, but sweet Mary had already cleaned it for me. I sat down and leaned to the side of it and laid my head on the little thin arm, shut my eyes, and fell asleep. I was surprised when I awakened early the next morning because I did not expect to have fallen asleep after the horrible day I had spent yesterday. I raised up and got my eyes focused and started to help Mary to prepare something for everyone to eat.

John came over and sat down on the floor right beside my chair. He said that he has just remembered something that Jesus had told the disciples the last time that they had sat and talked together. It was just a little while before He had gone to the Garden to pray. He said that they were just talking about the Father and His unconditional love for man, and Jesus looked at them and said these words: "As the Father hath loved me, so have I loved you: continue ye in my love. This is my commandment, that ye love one another, as I have loved you. Ye are my friends, and Greater love hath no man than this, that a man lay down his life for his friends" (John 15:9-13).

There have been many times that John has told me some of his favorite stories about his walk with Jesus. Each of the disciples has so many amazing memories that they have shared with me over the past few months. They have all come in from time to time to check on me and to see if I am well. I don't see them nearly as often as I would like because they are all going from place to place preaching and teaching in the name of Jesus Christ, the Savior, and the resurrected Son of God. They are carrying on the work that Jesus left them and commanded them to do.

Chapter 16

He Has Risen

It was the third day after the crucifixion of Jesus and the first day of the week. The Sabbath had already passed and Mary Magdalene and I, along with a couple of other women who had been faithful followers of Jesus, had bought some sweet spices and were going to the sepulcher to anoint His body. We wanted to go very early, the next morning, just before sunrise. We were worried about how we could roll away the huge stone that had been placed in front of the tomb.

The Roman soldiers wanted it sealed so that no one could go in. Knowing that Jesus had prophesied that He would rise in three days, they believed that some of His followers would come to the tomb and steal His body and then they would claim that He had risen, just as He had said that He would do. The soldiers felt that His disciples would do anything to keep His memory and His ridiculous teaching alive. These evil men had crucified Him, and yet His being dead still was not enough to satisfy their hatred for Him.

Pilate had ordered that two soldiers be placed on guard at the tomb of Jesus twenty-four hours a day until the three days that he had claimed to resurrect from the dead had long past. He said that they could split the time into two or three shifts and this he felt would certainly detour anyone from trying to steal the body.

The angel of the Lord came and put a deep sleep over the soldiers who were on guard that day, so that they would not see what was taking place in the tomb. He also had also rolled back the large stone because Jesus had risen and He had left. The poor men were facing certain death because of having gone to sleep during their time to be on watch.

Mary got up very early, long before the light of day. She said that she could not sleep, and not wanting to awaken the rest of us, she had decided to go ahead and get started with the anointing of the body again with spices. She had forgotten about the huge stone until she saw the sepulcher was open. She learned later that an angel had rolled the stone away. It was said that this angel, Gabriel's countenance, was like lightning and his raiment as white as snow. When the guards saw him, they dropped over and became as dead men.

Mary had not looked very far into the tomb, and she did not see the angel because when she had seen that the stone had been moved, she ran to find Jesus's disciples. First, meeting Peter and then saw John walking toward her and with tears streaming down her face, she said to them, "Peter, John, they have taken our Lord out of the tomb, and I know not where or why they have taken Him."

The two disciples and Mary turned around and ran back to the sepulcher and looked inside. Peter went in and saw the linen burial clothes were thrown over to the side but the napkin for His face had been folded and was lying neatly to the side.

The disciples knew that He had risen just as He had said and they left and went to their homes to patiently wait for Him to return to them. Mary did not leave at that moment. She, still weeping bitterly, walked over to the tomb and looking inside, saw two angels dressed in white. Both were sitting where Jesus had been laid: one at the head and the other at the feet.

And one of the angels said to her, "Woman, why do you weep?"

Mary answered and said, "Because they have taken my Lord and I know not where they have taken Him!" The angel answered her saying, "Fear not, I know whom seek ye. He is not here, for the Jesus who was crucified is now risen. Come and see the place where the Lord lay. Go quickly and tell his disciples that He has risen from the dead and if they will journey to Galilee, they shall see Him there."

As Mary turned to leave to go to tell the disciples, she saw a man standing in front of her. Since the area around the tomb was near a big beautiful garden, she assumed that the man must be the gardener.

She said, "Sir, I know you are the gardener and that you must be very busy, but if you have taken my Lord Jesus somewhere, please tell me where you have put Him. I will get some of His disciples to come and get His beloved body!"

Jesus said, "Mary!"

She said, "Master," for she recognized His voice.

She started to fall at His feet and worship Him but He said, "Mary, do not touch me because I have not yet ascended to my Father. Please go and notify the disciples that I have risen and I will see them in Galilee."

Mary left the sepulcher quickly and ran to find the disciples so that she could inform them of what the angel of the Lord had said to her and to tell them that she had seen Jesus! She met Peter and John along the way. After she had told them what Jesus had told her and about the angels, the three of them went on their way to find the other disciples and to tell them the glorious news.

As they hurried down the road, they met Jesus coming toward them. He said, "All hail." They recognized the voice and fell at His feet to worship Him. Jesus looking at them said, "Do not be afraid, just run and tell the other disciples to go to Galilee and there they shall find me waiting for them."

Now when the chief priest, Caiaphas, and his officers had heard that Jesus had risen, they were terrified that the Jews would find out. He knew that not only would they be laughed at and called fools, but they would be in a lot of trouble because they could not keep Him in the tomb. He also thought that depending on how angry Pilate would become; many of them could lose their lives.

All the priests and officers of Caiaphas immediately decided to call a council meeting. They secretly called the soldiers who had been on guard that morning to join them. When the soldiers had arrived, Caiaphas told them that they would be paid a great deal of money to keep this resurrection a secret. He said that they would have to lie, but in the long run, it could save their lives as well as the lives of the priests and their followers.

He told them to tell everyone that late that night, the disciples had sneaked into the tomb and stolen Jesus's body. The disciples wanted it to look as though this man had been a god and had risen just as He had said. The soldiers were also instructed to say that the disciples had taken the body to another city and hidden it somewhere out in the desert where it could never be found. These lies would put all the blame for the body's disappearance on the heads of the poor disciples and all the punishment would be theirs.

While the Jews were paying the soldiers to keep their secret, Jesus had gone to meet with His disciples. The doors to the room where the disciples had assembled and were waiting for Jesus had been shut and locked, for they still feared for their lives. The Jews were very furious and upset because the body was gone. Jesus appeared in their midst. He showed them His hands, His feet, and His side. When they had seen His wounds, they were so blessed to know that they had seen their Lord, who had risen in three days just as He had said. Kneeling at His feet, they worshiped Him and gave praise to God, His Father.

The last disciple to see Jesus was Thomas, for he had errands to run and although he had heard about the resurrection, it was eight days later before he saw Him. The other disciples just thought it was because he, as usual, was very much in doubt of what he had been told and was stalling for time because he didn't want to come.

Then coming into the room, where they had gathered once more, Thomas said, "I tell you now that until I touch the nail prints in His Hands and His feet, I will not believe that it is He! I don't care what the rest of you think has happened! I saw Him do many miraculous things, but His rising from the dead seems almost unachievable, even for Him!"

Then Jesus said, "Thomas come to me and touch my hands and thrust your hand into my side that you may believe." Thomas was still mumbling as he walked over to Jesus. After feeling His hands and His feet, and the marks that the old rusty spikes had left behind, he immediately fell to his knees and worshiped Him. Then in a very thunderous voice, with tears running down his face, he proclaimed, "My Lord and my God!"

Jesus said to him, "Thomas, seeing is indeed believing, but what about the man who believes without seeing. Being truly blessed, this man's home shall be in Glory with the Son and His Father."

Jesus spent a few more days visiting with His disciples and each time they saw Him they would fall on their knees and worship Him. Then, right before He left to go to the Father, He spoke to them saying:

"All power is given unto me in heaven and earth. Go ye therefore, and teach all nations, baptizing them in the name of the Father, and of the Son, and of the Holy Ghost" (Matt. 28:18, 19).

As He kept teaching them, he said to them: "Go into all the world, and preach the gospel to every creature. He that believeth and; he that believeth and is baptized shall be saved, but he that believeth not shall be damned."

Chapter 17

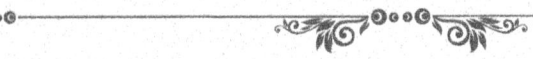

The Young Roman Soldier

About a week or so after Jesus had risen and gone back to His throne in Heaven, from where He came, everything was peaceful and quiet. I had just finished cleaning up and since no one was there but me, I decided to take my time working and maybe do some reminiscing about my "son." John had gone out to the temple to teach some young men; Mary and the others had gone to do several errands.

I really missed Jesus being here with me, and traveling along with Him to the cities and listening to His preaching and teaching. It was so awesome to watch as Jesus healed hundreds of people from every disease that had ever been known to man. I knew with all my heart where He had gone. One day when it comes time for me to face death, I know that I will see Him again and that I will live with Him throughout eternity. I could hardly wait for that time to come.

It was very warm in the house, and I decided to go outside and sit in the shade of the large olive tree. It had stood near the little brook for as long as I could remember. A cool, clean-smelling breeze was blowing and it was a very pleasant afternoon to be out in the fresh air. I had taken a blanket to sit on the hard ground. I leaned back against the tree and became so relaxed and comfortable that before I knew it, I had fallen asleep.

Suddenly, I was awakened by a strange noise. I sat up straight against the tree and looked over to my right. I saw a young, very tall, handsome man dismounting from the saddle of a beautiful brown horse. He was one of the Roman soldiers. I was too frightened to speak. My first thought was: he has come to arrest me, but for what reason? Could it be that I was the mother of the prophet Jesus whom they had crucified the week before? I knew that with the hatred that the cruel Roman soldiers felt for the Jewish people, we did not have to be guilty of anything. They would arrest one of us, only because we were a living and breathing Israelite.

Walking toward me, smiling, he extended his hand for a friendly handshake. "Mother of Jesus?" he asked.

"Yes," I said, "I was His mother!" He was a very polite young man and his smile showed a slight dimple in his chin. Then he said, "My name is Marcus and I have come to tell you the experience that I had with your 'son.' I thought that you might find it to be very comforting in your time of sorrow. After participating in His long tortuous death, I know who He is. He is truly the Christ, the only 'Begotten Son' of the only true living God, Jehovah."

Those words coming from a Roman soldier were very unusual because the Romans did not believe in our God, Jehovah. Suddenly, I was very interested in what this young soldier came to say. He sat down beside me on the blanket and began telling what was quite a lengthy, but truly astonishing experience for him and at the same time, it was a great blessing to me.

Marcus said that he had grown up believing that he owed his allegiance to Caesar only. He had been taught to hate all the Jewish people because he was told that all the Israelites were stupid, nasty people who were always arguing and fighting. They were trouble-makers and did not deserve to live for any reason except to be slaves, or to work for the Roman government and its people. He stated that from birth, all he had ever known was hatred, deceit, and cruelty, even from his parents and close family members. He believed as did all the other soldiers that his being a Roman soldier made him liken to a god. Under the Roman rulers, he had learned that he had the power and the authority to do anything that he wanted to do. However, he must be sure that his loyalty was first and foremost to Caesar.

Marcus said that he had always loved to watch crucifixions. His parents had taken him to see many. He remembered that even as a young child, he was always laughing at the poor man or woman who was hanging there. Later when he had become a soldier, he had been chosen to be a part of these horrible deaths. A couple of times, he had participated in the senseless and inhumane beating of the accused who was very often an innocent man like Jesus. The accusers may only have found fault with them because of their being an Israelite and would insist that they be punished by hanging on a cross.

Once, he was so happy because he had been chosen to carry the club to the cross of a man who was suspected of treason and plotting against Caesar. He was ordered to break his legs so that he would quickly die. Marcus said that he had laughed himself to tears while with each blow, the poor, dying man kept screaming out in more pain and agony.

He was the soldier who was chosen to break the legs of Jesus. Nevertheless, when he walked up to the middle cross, for some reason, he found to his surprise that he was glad that the man, Jesus was already dead. There would be no reason for him to break His legs.

He had heard all about the Jewish prophet Jesus from his fellow soldiers, but he had never been assigned to the area where He would be preaching. He had never met this man Jesus, heard him speaking, or even seen Him, but he had developed an intense hatred for Him. The only reason that he had to hate Him was from all the ridiculous and unbelievable things that he had heard. Anyone would be a skeptic. This man, Jesus, was a self-made, superhuman, and not only that, He also claimed to be the "God"!

At first, in my heart and mind, I wasn't sure where his story was going to end, but I was really concerned with the outcome. I was so stunned by the things that Marcus was describing to me that I needed to hear everything he had to say. Although, it seemed that he was possibly confessing something to me that he had done to Jesus, I had to know why this young Roman soldier had sought me out and was telling me all this. He did not seem hateful or arrogant, or to be bragging about the specifics of what he had done. If anything, it seemed that he was humbled by it all.

When he would speak the name of Jesus, I didn't hear any hatred for my "son" in his voice. He had spoken the entire time with a soft tone and a cheerful smile on his face.

He continued to tell me the reason that he had come to see me. He had heard that one of the Prophet's chosen disciples, a man called Judas Iscariot, had promised to betray Him to the chief priests for thirty pieces of silver. Marcus wanted to see the plans that the officers had for Jesus and what was going to happen to Him. It seemed that he had a chance not only to see this Jesus, but in his cruel mind, "justice" done. At the same time, he could put the idea of a Jewish rebellion down, before it could be started. Caesar would become very angry if something was not done with the troublemaker, Jesus of Nazareth.

A lot of the people, Israelites and soldiers as well, would ultimately be held accountable for all the "troublemakers." These were the ones who believed that they could crown the Prophet Jesus "king of the Jews." Many would be killed during the uprising and the rest of them would be imprisoned and put to death later for their taking part in the riot.

Late in the afternoon, of the day that Jesus was arrested, Marcus stopped a man on the roadside. He asked him if he had seen the Prophet Jesus, the man who claimed to be "God Himself." The man told him that he had heard that Jesus and a few of His disciples had gone to the Garden of Gethsemane for their evening prayers. Marcus said that he was just killing time because he had been given leave for a couple days. He decided to go to see for himself what was going to be occurring in the Garden.

At the same time, some of the Jewish leaders, the high priest's captain and a band of his officers were on their way to the Garden to arrest "the false prophet," who was known as Jesus of Nazareth. Marcus would have been more than happy to join them, but he was wearing his soldier uniform, the only clothes that he had. The fate of this man was in the hands of the Jewish leaders and not the Roman soldiers. Therefore, he did not have the authority to step in. He noticed from a distance that the disciple Judas Iscariot was with them at the head of the line. He was carrying a small money bag that was probably already filled with silver coins that he had been paid for betraying the man who had been his friend.

A few yards from the Garden, the band passed a couple of sleeping disciples along the way. Since Judas knew where to find Jesus, the band did not stop to awaken them to ask any questions. Up the path a few yards further, they found Jesus kneeling by huge rock praying. They stood silently watching Him for a moment. Sensing their presence, He stood and turned to face them.

Immediately, Judas the betrayer walked over to Him and as he kissed Him on the cheek, he said, "Hail, Master."

Then Jesus asked, "Whom do you seek?"

"Jesus of Nazareth," the leaders all said in unison.

"I am He!" answered Jesus. Then He said, "I have been with you in the temple and on the banks of the river. I have even eaten a meal with some of you in your homes and now, you come to me with staves and swords."

Then the captain of the band and the officers seized Jesus by the shoulders and bound Him and led Him away to Pilate, the Roman governor of Judea.

Trying to stay out of sight, Marcus followed the crowd to Pilate's hall, where Jesus would be condemned to die the cruel death on the old rugged cross. The governor did not want to order Him killed because he knew that Jesus was innocent of all the charges. He only wanted to scare Him enough so that he would stop preaching. All the multitudes of people who were following Him were believing the ridiculous claims that He had been making. They faithfully had accepted His lies as being the truth. Pilate, confident that his plan would work, ordered Jesus to be scourged with the normal torture tool, the cat of nine tails.

Then Pilate turned to the Jewish officers and high priest and asked, "What should I do with this Jesus of Nazareth after they had scourged Him?" They insisted on His being crucified.

When Pilate saw that he could convince them that Jesus was guilty of no crimes, he asked for a pan of water and washed his hands saying that he would not be a part of this. The Jewish leaders kept insisting that Jesus be crucified. Pilate was the only person who had the authority to order this death sentence, so he gave the order and the soldiers took Jesus to the whipping stocks to begin the punishment.

Marcus could not understand his feelings for this man. All the times before when a criminal was sent to be punished, he was willing and able to join the fun. Somehow, this time was different because this man Jesus was innocent. He was not guilty of anything, especially treason. The young soldier had heard that He had healed people, made the lame to walk, and had opened blinded eyes. On a couple of occasions, he had learned that Jesus had raised people from the dead. The Prophet was always doing everything that He did with love and compassion. Marcus could not understand why, His people, would hate Him so much.

Any other time, Marcus said that he would have gladly taken the cat of nine tails and torn the bloody flesh from the body of the accused. However, this time, he felt almost heartbroken. He could not imagine having this kind of feelings for anyone, much less an insane Jewish Prophet. He was the man who was causing so much trouble, claiming that He was the only "Begotten Son" of the God of heaven.

Finally, when the man's body became so grotesquely mangled and mutilated that it did not even look human, Marcus could no longer watch. He had to go to the back of the crowd; he simply could not bear the torture any longer. He said that you could hear Jesus's flesh tearing as the pieces of rock and metal ripped open His back.

He was beaten so horribly that His body looked like a gruesome bloody mess.

Marcus pretended to have heard a ruckus at the back line of the spectators, so that the other soldiers and officers would not realize that he was feeling sorry for this man. Many of the other people were beginning to leave because they obviously did not want to see the punishment as badly as they had thought that they did. It was truly more than an average man could stand to watch. The scourging of Jesus was absolutely the most brutal that Marcus had ever witnessed in his young life; he had seen and been a partaker of many of them. The poor man Jesus would stumble and, without making a sound, struggle and stand up for more. It looked as if it was not going to stop until He was dead. Then the captain of the guards told the soldier that He had enough. They didn't want to beat Him to death because Pilate had only wanted Him scourged, not killed.

Then the soldiers became angry and decided to stop the beating. Wanting to "get it over with," they could go afterward, get drunk, feast, party, talk, and joke about the execution as they had always done. With Jesus, the talk would be a lot worse. The man who had beaten Him, would be bragging about silencing the prophet who claimed that He was to be the King of the Jews forever. For the past three and a third years, this had been their goal, and now they had finally accomplished what they had wanted to do all the time.

Poor Marcus, although he hadn't touched the man or His cross, and he had done nothing but stand and watch, said that he felt as guilty as if he had done it all by himself.

He stayed near the crosses. He said that the saddest part of all for him was knowing that the two other men hanging there with Jesus were criminals. The man who was hanging on his left was a thief, and the one on His right had committed murder. Jesus who was hanging on the cross in the middle was innocent. The two criminals were barely beaten because the soldiers wanted to save all the "fun" as they had called it for Jesus. He was beaten so badly that He didn't look human and had suffered enough for all three of them.

Before they had hung Jesus on the cross, one of the soldiers had platted a crown of thorns and slapped it on His head. Some of the others had stripped Him and put a purple robe on Him and then they put a reed in His right hand. Having done that, they bowed to Him and mocked Him saying, "Hail, King of the Jews!" Then they spit on Him, right in the face, and took the reed and hit Him with a very violent lick to His head, making the thorns dig deep into his scalp. Blood and pieces of His flesh spurted everywhere and ran down His face and into His eyes, and some of it ran down onto the kingly robe that they had put on him. After they had mocked Him, they took off the purple robe and put His bloody loin cloth back on Him. Then they led Him away to be crucified.

Jesus called out from the cross, "Father, forgive them for they know not what they do!" Those words tore at the very heart of Marcus and he turned and ran down the road. He ran just a few yards, when he had to turn around and hurry back. It seemed that he was being drawn back to Jesus and to the foot of the cross. When he returned, most of the people who had been standing there the entire time had left. Many of Jesus's disciples had run away earlier fearing for their lives. Marcus said that he had immediately fallen on his knees at the cross and put his head right at the feet of Jesus. Touching His bloody right foot with his fingertips, he then asked Jesus Christ for forgiveness of all his sins. He had no question that He was "God in the flesh." Everything that He had said was true.

He said that he then felt the Holy Spirit come over him, and when he stood up, all the hatred that he had known in his life was gone. He told me it was as if he had "left the old soldier at the foot of the cross and a new man had emerged." Suddenly, he felt a peace and joy in his heart that he had never before known.

He had to find the "earthly mother" of Jesus and share with her the experience that he had at the feet of her "son," who he knew was surely the "Son of God"! There were many people that day who realized exactly who He was. Even one of the men who were hanging on the cross beside Jesus had asked Him if He would please remember him when He came into His kingdom.

Standing close to the cross, Marcus had heard Jesus tell the man that very day he would be with Him in paradise.

Oh yes, he said, many lives were changed that day. When the man Jesus gave up His Spirit to God the Father, and the mighty earthquake shook the whole world and ripped everything apart, surely everyone standing there knew that He was truly "the Son of God"!

When Marcus had finished talking, he looked over at me and smiled. Then the two of us stood up against the big tree where we had been sitting the whole time that he was giving me his testimony of his new joy-filled life. He then reached down and picked up my blanket, folded it into a small wad, and handed it to me. Then he leaned over and gave me a hug, and without a word, he walked over to his horse. It had silently stood in the same spot, not moving even its head. Marcus rubbed its nose, adjusted the saddle, mounted up, and smiled at me again as he waved goodbye and rode out of sight.

I was surprised that this young Roman soldier had just come to me and had acted as though he had known me most of his life, and we were best friends. He was so respectful toward me and just an exceptional young man. He neither acted nor looked anything like I thought the brawny, unshaven, cutthroat Roman soldiers to be.

I felt as if Jesus had been to visit with me. Marcus was right. I was truly comforted and blessed by his coming here to share his experience with me. I was so happy that this outstanding young man's eyes had been opened to the truth. I went into the house, lit the lamp just long enough to get myself ready to go to bed. I turned down the covers, fluffed them up a bit, took a few sips of water, then I quickly blew out the light and laid down. I had a long, peaceful, night's sleep, the first good rest that I had gotten since the crucifixion.

From that day, I have had many visits from people whom I had never met, telling me about the differences that Jesus had made in their lives. Although I have never had one quite like the meeting that I had with Marcus, the young Roman soldier.

The disciples, especially Peter, James, Matthew, and Thomas, would stop in just to say hello and to make sure that I was well. They all knew that John had moved me into a room in his home, so that he could do as Jesus had asked while He was hanging on the cross. He had planned to take care of me for the rest of my life.

My dear friend, Mary, was always somewhere close by. Everyone was amazed when I told them the story of Marcus and the change that Jesus had made in his life. Sadly, I never saw or heard from the young man again.

Chapter 18

My "Son" No More, but "My Lord and My God"

Tonight, I am more lonely and heartbroken than I could have ever imagined would have been possible. I have to say that my "son" as I knew Him as a human is, now my "son" no more. I feel empty as a mother, yet filled to the brim as a cup that is running over. Although, I am physically and emotionally hurting, I am spiritually Blessed beyond measure. Jesus has now taken His rightful place back on the throne to the right of His Father, God. He has fulfilled His destiny from whence He came to earth. My "son" is now my Lord and my God and my Savior. He is the Son of God and the Lord of All Creation. I had so many memories that came to my mind last night, now that His life as a man was over and done. While desperately trying to get some sleep, I began to remember a lot of things that I had forgotten over the past thirty-three and one third years.

During the long sleepless night, I found myself comparing the torn mangled adult body of my Lord and my God, Jesus, to that of my young "son," Jesus. Before I was ready to get up, the early morning light began to beam into my front door, straight to the chair where I was sitting, and into my face. I smiled and thanked my God for the gift of His Son. Yes, I had a restless night, but all in all, a very blessed and comforting one. I felt very refreshed, even though I hadn't slept a wink.

I can't see Him or touch Him like I could when He was here in the flesh walking with me, but I know that He has risen from the dead. He is as much alive now as He was then and He is still in my heart. My "son" no more, but now, today, my Lord and my God. Knowing this to be a fact is the only way that I can live the rest of my life, with my "son" not physically here with me, but in heaven on His throne.

When I began my night of comparison, naturally, I just started at the "top" of His body and with His precious head. Jesus had been laughed at and mocked so many times. The crown of thorns that was placed on His head was the worse mockery of them all because it was also another way to torture and poke fun at Him.

I thought of those cruel, piercing thorns and the humiliating sign that was hanging over His head, "King of the Jews." If only Governor Pontius Pilate, who had carved the letters himself and those poor people who were standing there with him at the time, had known the truth as I did. Blood was pouring down Jesus's precious face, into his eyes, and down into His mouth and nose and was dripping down on His chest. His face was so gory and His hair was caked with blood. Yes, His face had been badly beaten. One of the men had punched Him a couple of times, in the nose and mouth. He had been spit upon, and His usually bright sparkling and compassionate eyes were almost swollen shut due to the horrendous beating that He had taken. His mouth was bleeding and His lips looked as if they had been turned inside out. There were big holes in His face where the cruel soldier had yanked His beard out by the hands full. The pores were left bleeding and open and His facial skin was so chafed that it was a blistered red. Then I began to compare the mangled head and face of the Man Jesus, to the dear angelic boy face of my "son," Jesus. His eyes were always so sparkling bright and His little face glowed as if there were a halo hanging above His head. I would wash His sweet smiling face, comb His black hair, and kiss His rosy cheeks.

Sometimes I patted His head and mussed up His hair just to tease Him. He would smile and giggle. My mind kept going back to the hideous crown of thorns that cut into His forehead like a bunch of little stabbing sharp knives. They had made his face so grotesquely bloody that it would have been unrecognizable, even to me. I had been there with Him throughout the entire ordeal and knew it was "my" son, who was hanging on that cruel, rough, splintery, cross.

Next, I began to compare His mouth. From the loving adorable baby mouth that giggled and smiled all the time, to the adult mouth that spoke with great power and glory. The same mouth that called out and rebuked unclean evil spirits, had the capability and authority from Father God to call Lazarus up from the dead. Those lips had preached repentance to thousands of multitudes of followers. The same sacred Holy adult mouth that had uttered from the cross in unconditional love, "Father, forgive them for they know not what they do." What a precious mouth indeed!

Then I thought of His heart, that no human eyes could ever see inside, it had been broken into millions of pieces, so many times. It was crying out not because of the pain and agony that He was suffering physically. It was crying out, from the mental anguish, knowing that His people could be so cruel not only to Him, but to anyone.

Then I came to the most important part of all. I began to compare His Glorious godly hands. They were always so smooth and soft for a man's hands. Although, He had helped me in my vegetable garden and had worked in carpentry, they weren't calloused or scarred. Not until now of course and both of His hands are nail scarred because they were nailed to the cross. The spikes were in the joint at the hand and wrist area. His hands were stretched out shoulder-length and the soldiers had driven a rusty old spike that was about six inches long into each of them. They had ripped through His precious flesh as they were nailed into the wood.

The hands of Jesus played a big part in who He was and in His ministry. These were the same loving hands that as a child, He had held the dove, that had broken its neck, up to His Father. The same hands that had patted my face and said, "I love you, Mother Mary!" The same sweet baby hands that He, would clap every time that he would be happy or get the least bit excited.

And then, the same hands that had grown, from precious little baby hands, into the beautiful passionate hands of a loving "God" man. These were the healing hands of the one and only man, who truly loved the entire world unconditionally!

The powerful hands that had touched the eyes of those who were blind and made them see, and the lips of those who were dumb and made them talk. They had touched the ears of the deaf and made them hear, and the legs of the lame and made them walk. Then I remembered something else that I had almost forgotten. It was just after the Crucifixion. Everyone had left and it was just a few minutes before John and Mary had taken me home to get some rest. John had pointed out to me, a man who was standing near the cross crying bitterly. He said that he was the same man, who was with the group in the Garden of Gethsemane that came to arrest Jesus. He was also a captain in the band of the followers of the high priest. A disciple of Jesus had become furious and had grabbed a sword out of one of the officer's belts and slashed off the man's right ear. The wrathful disciple who had cut off his ear was Peter. Jesus had scolded Peter, as he had done so many times. He then reached down, picked up the man's ear, and put it back into place on the side of his face; even though the man had meant to harm Him. The man's name was Malchus. As I watched him standing there, I remember thinking; that man has realized the identity of the man who is hanging on the cross in the middle. Yes, the Lord Jesus had used His hands then, to show love to a man who hated Him.

The hands of Jesus were a very important and memorable part of Him. He has used them to reach down and raise the dead and make them live again. His powerful hands could calm the raging sea. He always lifted His hands up to His Father and gave Him the Glory and Praise before and after every miracle that He ever performed. There had been thousands of miracles during His three and one third years in the ministry. But now as I make my loving comparisons, I can't help thinking again about His blood caked hands being nailed to that old cross in shame and disgrace like a common criminal. Yet He was innocent of every crime of which He had been accused.

Then I compared His back and shoulders. Beaten beyond recognition, if you could see them without seeing the rest of the body at the same time then, you would think you were looking at a rare piece of meat. A part of His intestines, was hanging out of a large hole that was made in His back by the soldier who had been scourging him with the cat of nine tails.

Each time that he had hit Him, the cracking whip had ripped out big hunks of "bloody flesh."

This was the same little back that I rubbed and patted, as I was rocking Him to sleep, when He was just a baby. The same back now grownup, mangled and gory, that as He walked up the hill of Calvary, had carried that old rugged cross and the sins of the entire world.

Last but just as important, are those precious feet. Except for occasionally taking a boat over to the other side of the river, Jesus's only means of transportation was walking. He never owned a horse or a donkey. Many times, when Jesus would stop by the house, His feet would be so blistered that they would be oozing with some watery infection from the long journey that He had just made. He made these trips every day; preaching, teaching, and healing everyone who needed Him. Sadly, some of the people still hated Him, although He had cured the infirmities of either them or a member of their families.

These were the same feet that were nailed to the cross with one foot slightly over the other by one old nine inch, rusty spike. I can't stress to you enough that the spikes in His hands and His feet were to hold Him on the cross. Little did the crowd know that His love for mankind is what kept Him hanging up there for more than six hours. The old rusty nails stood for humiliation and humbleness for the world to see. Not having the spiritual power from Father God it would have been impossible for those cruel men to take His dear life. He freely gave it as a sacrifice so that the entire world could be saved and live forever in heaven with Him and the Father.

These were the same feet that as a very young boy were always dirty. I would get so tickled at Him because the rest of His body and His clothes would be spotlessly clean. His little feet, even if He was wearing sandals, would be filthy. Being a typical boy, Jesus never walked around anything including a mud puddle. He would step in the water because when the weather was hot, it would be very cooling to Him. He had the cutest, most precious, tiny, fat baby feet. Joseph and I would nibble and kiss His toes. We loved to watch Him get tickled. He would giggle and laugh and then He would curl them. After that we would let them go.

Remembering that as a baby, His precious little feet were so sensitive, just seeing the old rusty spikes in His adult feet had split my heart wide open. He was the most honest, loving man, who ever walked the face of the earth. However, in their hatred and their disbelief, the poor Jewish people had cried out to Governor Pilate and had convinced him to crucify the Jewish Messiah.

Thinking back to the old rugged cross that Jesus was hanging on in such shame and disgrace, brings heart-felt suffering to me. He who had committed no crime; yet His punishment was more severe than that of a thief and a murderer. He who had committed no sin, yet He had suffered so hideously for the sins of the world. He who showed only love and compassion to every person whom he ever met, yet was treated with so much hatred. Only the great love of the only begotten "SON of God," could and would, have taken on this fate for the entire human race so that it could be saved. It was not the old rusty spikes and the ropes that held Him to that old rugged cross; it was love that held Him up there—"HIS UNCONDITIONAL LOVE" for the entire world!

John and I have shared many unforgettable memories about Jesus. I was not there at the Last Supper. I did not see Him as He had humbly washed the feet of the eleven disciples. When he went to the Garden of Gethsemane to pray to God, His Father, I did not go with Him. I did not witness the inhumane acts of the brutal men who came to arrest Him, but I have been told about those heinous events that took place in the Garden. John, Peter, and James, three of His most trusted disciples, had all seen and testified that these facts were the truth. These men loved Him as much as I did. They had worshipped Him because they all had been shown by the Holy Spirit that Jesus was indeed, the Christ, the Son of the Living God.

I had told John all about Jesus from the beginning, and about all the encounters that Joseph and I had with the angel, Gabriel. I also talked about a lot of fond memories that only a mother would keep locked safely in her heart. We would sometimes talk late into the night, sharing our special and amazing memories about Him. Our talking seemed to be good therapy for both of us in our time of grief. These occasions helped both of us to be able to bear the lonesomeness of His not being with us right now, and to get us through these past few weeks.

I had finally realized after all these years, that Jesus was indeed, *born to die a "bloody death!"* His precious blood had to be shed for the salvation of the world, because without the blood, there can be no remission of sin. *Jesus was our blood atonement!* I did not fully understand this fact until, after the crucifixion and then the resurrection had taken place. Today, when I think of His entire life that I shared with Him, as my "son" while He walked the earth in human form, I can truly say, without any question that I was: blessed among women! I could and I do worship "my son" who is my "son" no more, but my "Lord and my God"!

References

King James Version Super Giant Print Reference Bible (1996). Nashville, Tennessee: Broadman and Holman.
The Merriam-Webster Thesaurus (2005). Springfield, Massachusetts: Merriam-Webster, Inc.

About the Author

Paulette Sizemore and her husband, Basil have been happily married for forty-eight years. They have three children, eight grandchildren, and three great-grandchildren. Paulette loves to write. She has written twenty-three gospel songs, several short stories, and has had one of her poems published. The poem was written about one of her infant granddaughters.

Basil has a passion for music. A few years ago, the Sizemore family's gospel singing group and band were known as the Amazing Grace Trio.

The trio sang at several small churches in the Knoxville area. Since the children have grown up and married, the singing has more or less come to a standstill. However, they sing at their home church where their younger daughter's husband, James, is the pastor. On special occasions, they all gather at Basil and Paulette's home for one of mama's home-cooked meals and then after eating do some "picking and grinning."